Count it all

Joy!

WELLNESS AND FAITH:
A *STUDY IN JAMES*

JOYCE AINSWORTH
&
JUNE CHAPKO

FOREWORD

Our desire is for you to develop a personal journey to real wellness. We want you to experience the freedom that comes from an intimate relationship with Jesus Christ, and witness His love for you through reading your Bible, studying the Word and through prayer. To this end, we have designed each day's study to help you discover the truths of the Bible, guide you to making positive changes in your mind and body, and strengthen and encourage you. As you begin making baby steps in your journey, God will begin transforming your life.

We encourage you to begin the process of keeping a written record of this journey. You will slowly start seeing the truth in the phrase Change Your Mind – Change Your Body – Change Your Life! Page by page, your recorded thoughts will spur a change in your body, which ultimately will change your life.

Our journey to wellness will not please the devil. The path we will travel may at times seem hard, bringing difficult circumstances. We may be tempted to turn back, or worse, give up. Life change takes courage and commitment but it doesn't mean we can't find joy along the way. Scripture reminds us to "Rejoice always, pray continually, give thanks in all circumstances; for this is God's will for you in Christ Jesus" (1 Thessalonians 5:16-18).

It is our prayer that He will bring joy to your heart so you may experience abundant life. God bless you as you begin this study, and our prayer is for you to *count it all joy*.

HOW TO USE THIS STUDY:

This study may be used individually or in a small group. It contains tools which will enable you to be successful in losing weight, overcoming obstacles and temptations, growing spiritually, and changing your life for the better. You can accomplish these things with joy throughout the journey. Use each of the important tools found in this study to guide you toward a balanced and healthy life.

- Journaling Pages: Day seven of each of the ten weeks is a journaling page. You will find a journal prompt at the top to help you reflect on what God has taught you that week. Please utilize this tool. It will draw you closer to the Lord as you write what's on your heart that day.

- Choose Your Challenge: These are things you can choose from to further your progress. Life Change is possible by the power of Christ, and yet, He expects us to do our part. He empowers us as we step out of our comfort zone and face the challenge of the week.

- Affirmations: A huge part of your success will be seeing yourself successful. This can happen as you speak affirming things to yourself each day. Make copies on cards and post them in a visible place for you to speak out loud daily.

- Inner Reflections: After each day's study, you will find a reflection thought to help you digest what you studied that day. If you are doing this study on your own, the reflections may provide you food for thought or journaling ideas. If you are doing this study with others, you may find the daily reflection thoughts helpful for discussion during small group time.

CONTENTS

WEEK 1
JOYFUL ENCOUNTERS

Scripture Focus of the Week

Consider it pure joy, my brothers, whenever you face trials of many kinds

[James 1:2]

I remember seeing an old friend. Upon recognition we hugged tightly, squealing for joy at seeing each other again after such a long time. We caught each other up on information since last parting ways, and my sweet friend shared with me that she had cancer and was about to undergo treatment. I had prayer with her and we left, promising to keep in touch. Since that encounter, we have been meeting regularly and praying for healing. I try to take her a care box every week or so of healthy food items for her journey, just to encourage her during this difficult time in her life. She tells me often how good God is for renewing our friendship at just the moment she needed a friend the most. This sweet girl has stage IV cancer, and even though she has endured countless tests, treatments, and doctors' visits, she is still bursting at the seams filled with genuine thankfulness and joy.

Do you remember the childhood song "Joy in My Heart"? It is a catchy song with a lot of truth. My friend's spirit reminds me of this song and gives me renewed hope in all situations, even the most difficult ones.

The things and situations we encounter as we move along on our life journey could cause us to quit or get discouraged. On the other hand, if we have the joy of the Lord in our heart, those encounters can be times of joy as we overcome difficulty. Struggling to lose weight, become healthy, and live a well-balanced life has many challenges attached, but so does living a joy-filled life. As we begin our study in the book of James, may the Lord inspire us to dig deep and learn how to count it all joy!

DAY 1 ~ NOT IF, BUT WHEN

James doesn't say *if* we face trials, but *when* we face them. This points us to a clear assumption that trials are coming and it will be during these tests and challenges that our faith will grow and mature. Our Scripture this week encourages us to consider what kind of joy it is when we face trials.

____

Why do you think James emphasized *pure* when he described joy?

____

Pure joy is not dependent upon circumstances. It comes from God. We may feel joyful sometimes because nice things happen in our life or we're in a good mood, but the way to know if it's pure joy is if it's still there when trouble hits. We don't count it joy because of the trouble; no one welcomes trouble. We can have pure joy in the midst of it, though, knowing God takes care of us.

What kind of trials does James say that we should count as pure joy?

____

Look up the word *trials* and then write out your thoughts on the definition.

____

____

Hebrews 12:2-3 (KJV) says, "Looking onto Jesus the author and finisher of our faith; who for the joy that was set before him endured the cross, despising the shame, and is set down at the right hand of the throne of God. For consider him that endured such contradiction of sinners against himself, lest ye be wearied and faint in your minds."

What was the expectation Jesus had that allowed Him to endure the cross and shame?

____

____

____

He knew what was waiting for Him beyond His trial. He knew joy was coming, and it gave Him the endurance he needed. We too can have expectations of joy during the trials we face because Jesus is with us. Look for the positive because of what the trial can produce. James admonishes us to turn our hardships into times of perseverance.

Share a time when you experienced a hardship in your life and remained joyful. What was the struggle, and how did you praise God?

____

____

Look up 2 Corinthians 1:4-6 and identify who comforts us when we are experiencing trials.

____

____

Pure joy can result as we allow God to be our comfort in and through all our trials and troubles. When others ask, "How did you get through that?", we can say, "Only with the strength of God."

Consider the following list of trials and circle any you have experienced.

Abuse

Addiction (alcohol, drugs, food, etc.)

Bankruptcy

Death of a Loved One

Divorce

Loss of a Relationship

Loss of a Job

Natural Disaster

Rebellious child

Health Issues (diabetes, arthritis, high blood pressure, etc.)

Other: ____

Let's review 2 Corinthians 1:4 and write why God comforts us in all our troubles.

____

____

Enduring joy is the result as we allow God to use each trial and trouble in our lives to teach us how to be the encouragement and comfort for others.

In closing today, review the list of trials on previous page that you circled and then consider ways that you can comfort and encourage others experiencing similar trials. List several actions of encouragement you can give. Pray about whom God wants you to encourage.

____

____

____

____

Inner Reflection: Consider a recent/current trial in your life. Do you think your reaction to it glorified God? What do you think was the purpose of the trial?

DAY 2 ~ PERSEVERANCE

James served with a constant threat of persecution, as did many of the early church leaders during this time. The practical teaching in James guides us to trust God in the most difficult situations. Our true character is seen and reflected through the day-to-day challenges we face.

Look up the following passages and write down the common thought expressed in each one.

Romans 5:3-5   ____

2 Corinthians 6:3-7 ____

2 Peter 1:2-9   ____

We see that all these verses deal with perseverance. Just as James said, tough times can teach us perseverance. We can't really know the depth of our character until we see how we react under pressure. It is easy to be kind and loving when everything is going well and life is easy, but can we be kind when we are being treated unfairly, have been intentionally wronged by someone, or experience other trials? What is inside our heart will determine how we react to tough times that hit us on the outside.

Describe a time when you wanted to quit when you were going through a difficult time. How did you respond at the beginning, during, and end of it? Why do you think you were tempted to quit?

____

____

Read Colossians 1:11-12 and answer the following questions.

Why are we strengthened? (vs. 11)

____

Strengthening certainly doesn't happen on our own. It comes about according to God's glorious might. He strengthens us with hope so we will have great endurance, perseverance, and patience to go through whatever kind of trial is in our life at the time.

How should we respond to God's strengthening? (vs. 12)

____

Just as the title of this study ("Count it all Joy") says, we should respond by giving joyful thanks to the Father. A response of joyful thanks means we admit our dependence on Him and our trust in Him.

What do we receive from God? (vs. 12)

____

By enduring and persevering through the trials in life, by counting it all joy, and by giving joyful thanks to the Father, we are qualified to share in the inheritance of His holy people in the kingdom of light.

The hard places in our wellness journey give us an opportunity to grow dependent on God and His strength. Tough choices we have to make every day teach us to hold on to Him as if our very life depends on it. The raw truth is that your life does depend on it.

My struggle with food has been a hard place in my life for most of my life. Even today, I can allow the counting, measuring, and tracking of food and exercise choices to become burdensome and steal my joy, but I refuse to allow it to be my choice. A joyful response to God for allowing me the ability to make better choices opens the door of freedom, allowing His strength to empower me.

Close your study time today by writing out a prayer of praise to God for the times you struggle the most in your wellness journey.

____

____

____

____

Inner Reflection: What has been the most difficult thing you've encountered when it comes to persevering through a trial? Think about the steps you took to come through it.

DAY 3 ~ BECOMING MATURE

Yesterday we talked about how God allows troubles of all kinds for our good and how the testing of our faith develops perseverance. Today, let's look at the aspect of becoming mature. Read James 1:4 and write in your own words what this Scripture says about maturity.

____

____

Becoming spiritually mature begins following salvation. It is an ongoing process and often requires a radical reordering of one's priorities. It is impossible to mature spiritually apart from the Word of God.

Look up 1 Peter 2:2 and fill in the blanks.

"Like ______________ ____________, crave _________________ milk, so that by it you may ___________ up in your salvation."

After salvation, a Christian begins the growth process. Just like babies need milk to grow up strong, Christians start out on spiritual milk of the Word. We need the pure doctrine of the Gospel. How do we get it? By hearing it preached and reading the Word of God.

Turn to 1 Corinthians 3:2. What kind of food comes after spiritual milk?

____

After being on spiritual milk, a Christian will begin requiring solid food. Meat is needed for strength. If we are to be spiritually strengthened to become mature in our faith, we need the meat of the Word. We will only get that if we dig in and ask God to give it to us.

Read Hebrews 6:1.

Once we pass the milk stage and move on to the meat, we don't want to go back to the elementary teachings and begin laying the foundation of repentance again in our life.

Why do you think God want us to move on and become mature?

____

Being mature does not mean we are insulated from pain. It means God will be close, will give us the strength to endure, and will help us grow through the struggles in our lives.

Spiritual maturity will be seen through the joy that believers display as they become doers as well as hearers of the Word.

The process of spiritual maturity is achieved by becoming more like Jesus Christ every day. After salvation, every Christian begins a personal process of spiritual growth—daily striving to become spiritually mature.

Take some time to consider some specific ways that will help you become spiritually mature during this study.

____

____

____

How will becoming spiritually mature help you handle the temptations that come into your wellness journey daily?

____

____

____

Inner Reflection: Think about spiritual maturity. What indications can you list that show you have matured in the past few years?

DAY 4 ~ DOUBLED-MINDED

In the Dr. Doolittle stories, there is an animal with a head at either end of its body. It was always trying to walk in two directions at once. The animal was called a *pushmi-pullyu*. This is an excellent example of a double-minded person.

We have so many resources available to us that can provide answers and understanding to our questions about the Bible and our faith. Unfortunately, we may have such an abundance that it causes us to become uncertain about what is true and what is misguided teaching. One day we might think one way, but after reading or hearing a different opinion, we change our mind. We're pushed one way and pulled in another. We know that God is not the author or confusion, so let's look at how we can avoid becoming a double-minded person.

Let's begin today by reading James 1:5-8.

What does verse 8 say about being double-minded?

____

James describes one who is indecisive in prayer as "a _______-_______ man, _________ in all his ways."

The Greek word translated "double-minded" is *dipsuchos* , from *dis*, meaning "twice", and *psuche*, meaning "mind". James uses it to describe someone who is divided in his interests or loyalties, wavering, uncertain, two-faced, and half-hearted.

A mind that wavers is not completely convinced that God's way is best. At times we want to treat God's Word like human advice. This wavering between worldly and godly wisdom causes us to be double-minded, which makes us ask, "Are we really making the right decision?"

Explain a time when you may have questioned God's plan. What struggles did you encounter when making the decision?

____

____

Read Matthew 21:21-22.

Doubt and uncertainty in our communication with God short-circuits our relationship with Him. In Matthew 21:21-22, what does Jesus tell us we must do? What should we not do?

____

Before asking God for anything, we should first ask ourselves questions that directly bear on our prayers…

Is my request in opposition to God's Word?

Is this something that will hinder my spiritual growth?

How will I respond to God if He says no?

The right answers will affect our prayer life in a powerful and effective way.

Have you ever considered yourself double-minded in your prayer life?

____

____

A couple of ways we can help prevent becoming double-minded:

1. What does Psalm 119:105 say the Word of God is for us? How does the Word of God impact your decision making?

____

____

2. Don't waste your life because of fearful indecisions. What decisions are you fearful of making at this time?

____

____

Don't be fearful about making decisions. Think about how many times it says in the Bible to "fear not". There are enough "fear not" places in God's Word for you to have one each day of the year. Yes, 365 times it says, "fear not".

James says that a doubting person is "like a wave of the sea, blown and tossed…unstable in all he does." When we doubt, we become double-minded.

We cannot be both certain and doubting. To have the joy of peace, we must have faith and not doubt.

Inner Reflection: Am I prone to avoiding decisions because of fear? Do I fear failure or success?

DAY 5 ~ CONSIDER THE PURPOSE

Going through trials can draw some into a deeper dependency on God, while others react with anger toward God. A deeper dependency on God will help us get through our trial with less stress and fear, while lashing out at God in anger can bring more pain and distance us from Him. By considering the purpose of the various trials we face, we will stand a better chance of emerging from them with joy, peace, and strength.

Read James 1:12.

James echoes in verse 12 the thought begun in verse 2 where he called on believers to categorize hard times as pure joy. Why?

____

____

When we consider the purpose of our trials, we begin to see how our faith only grows stronger when tested. Trusting God through our trial pushes us toward the Christ-like maturity of trusting God more deeply, with greater endurance.

When we choose to keep trusting God in the midst of trials, troubles, and temptations, our faith and action brings His blessing. Our circumstances may be hard, but God is with us through life's most difficult moments.

Have you understood the purpose of a particular trial in your life? If so, explain how you discovered it.

____

____

What does the Bible say we will receive if we persevere under the trials of this life?

____

____

Look up the following Scriptures. What do they have in common?

Revelation 2:10 ____

1 Corinthians 9:24-27 ____

1 Peter 5:4 ____

2 Timothy 4:8 ____

The crown is an additional reward, given in eternity, for Christians who refused to stop trusting God even when their trials on earth became difficult. These believers trusted God through their trials instead of turning away. They loved God and continued to obey Him in their hardship.

It is important for us to remember that God's crown of life is not glory and honor here on this earth, but the reward of eternal life. Eternal life is not something we achieve; it is something we receive. This, my friend, is pure joy.

> **Inner Reflection: Can I see purpose in my trials? What is it? How does knowing (or not knowing) my purpose help or deter me to persevere?**

DAY 6 ~ STOP AND CONSIDER

This week on day four, we talked about being doubled-minded. As we stop and consider this for a moment, I am reminded again of the little animal in the Dr. Doolittle stories. There have been many times that I felt like the pushmi-pullyu. In my journey to wellness, it seemed I would take two steps forward and one step back, always being tossed to and fro, never moving as quickly in the right direction as I wanted to. In the very beginning, I wanted to lose weight, I needed to lose weight, and I was desperate to lose weight—but there I was asking, can I still eat fried chicken?

Now why would fried chicken even be on my mind? I was looking for a reason to give up right from the beginning. I had failed so long that it would be easier to quit rather than have another failed attempt at weight loss. I was double-minded in so many ways, and even today I have to watch out for the devil luring me back into a double-minded mindset. It is easy to be drawn in because I failed so long.

During the earlier days of my weight-loss journey, I learned that failure is final only when we don't get back up. I also came to realize that being double-minded is simply a lack of trust in God. When we trust and listen to God, failure can become an opportunity for life changing possibilities. I had to see the truth…yes, I could still eat fried chicken, but it's not something I could eat every day. As I began to pray about every decision concerning food, I realized God cared enough to direct me on food choices.

Today: Stop and consider possible areas in your journey where you may be double-minded. Consider how you might overcome them in these areas.

CHOOSE YOUR CHALLENGE FOR THE WEEK

NUTRITION CHALLENGE—GOAL: CHANGE YOUR MIND!

1. Forgo ground beef this week and use ground turkey instead!
2. Start the switch to nonfat milk: if you currently drink whole milk, move to 2%; if you drink 2%, move to 1%; and if you drink 1%, you are ready for nonfat. Try mixing it (use the step-down program; it works every time).
3. Skip the slice of cheese on your sandwich or try some different kinds of cheese, like a little bit of a hard flavorful variety like romano or provolone.

FITNESS CHALLENGE—GOAL: CHANGE YOUR BODY!

1. Five days this week, go for a 15-minute walk! Walk at whatever speed is comfortable. Just do it! Walk inside, outside, or around the living room or house. What about the shopping mall? Anywhere—just do it!
2. Start using a pedometer. This is an inexpensive tool that really helps you be mindful of how much you are walking or how much you need to walk.

LIFESTYLE CHALLENGE—GOAL: CHANGE YOUR LIFE!

1. Identify one source of stress that's easily erased and then do whatever is necessary to eliminate it. This could be as simple as clearing the clutter off your desk, getting a portion-control plate, packing your lunch the night before, keeping your gym bag in the car, or making a grocery list.

Challenge I Chose ~ Progress I Made:

DAY 7 ~ JOURNAL PROMPT:

I stand empowered by the Holy Spirit and need to be strengthened in…

WEEK 2
JOYFUL ENDURANCE

Scripture Focus of the Week

*When tempted, no one should say, "God is tempting me."
God cannot be tempted by evil, nor does he tempt anyone.*

[James 1:13]

I once had a wise lady tell me that temptation is enticing and attractive and will take me further than I want to go, keep me longer than I want to stay, and cost me more than I want to pay. There has never been a truer statement. If we look around, we see temptation on every corner. We are inundated with all sorts of temptation through the use of television and high-tech devices. It has become easier to be drawn to the onslaught of indulgences to our minds, bodies, and spirits. Many of us are struggling with the temptation of overindulgence in the area of food. It is easy to blame others and make excuses for evil thoughts and wrong actions; we love to shift the blame onto the shoulders of others for our lack of self-control. Let's face it—it is easier to blame others than it is to take responsibility ourselves.

This week, as we dig a little deeper into the book of James, we are going to explore the many facets of temptation and see what joyful living can look like in the face of daily temptation. James said we will all face temptation and our own evil desire will tempt us to sin but God is at work for our good and His glory. As we learn to identify who is really at the root of all temptation and begin to take the steps to overcome the battle, we will learn to count even this as joy!

DAY 1 ~ WHO'S TEMPTING WHO?

As we start our study this week, let's review our Scripture focus for the week. Write out James 1:13 here:

____

____

This verse says that God cannot be tempted by evil and that He does not tempt others. So where does temptation come from? Read James 1:14.

____

____

Temptation comes from evil desires inside us, and Scripture is clear it does not come from God. Temptation begins with a thought: we focus on fulfilling that unhealthy or evil desire. It becomes sin when we dwell on it to the point it becomes an action.

What does the word **tempted** mean?

____

____

To tempt is to test, try, prove, or solicit to evil. As used in our Scripture focus, tempted means a solicitation to evil. James clearly points out that this temptation is not from God but from man's own inner lust. No more blame can be placed on God. It is time for us to take responsibility for our actions.

Here are some common excuses used when we are tempted:

1. I just could not help it.

2. Everybody's doing it.

3. Nobody's perfect.

4. The devil made me do it.

Can you think of others? Write down one that you use on a regular basis?

____

____

When we make excuses, we are simply trying to shift the blame to someone or something else. As believers who desire real change, we need to accept responsibility for our behavior, confess our actions, and ask God for forgiveness.

We need to be reminded that God may test us but He does not tempt us by trying to seduce us to sin. He loves us and He is on and by our side. We can always resist temptation to sin by turning to God for strength.

My small group has been a strength builder for many years, teaching me to resist temptation in so many areas of my life by having a group of accountability buddies I can count on.

Another area has been menu planning. Planning meals has helped me stay on track and eat on time, allowing me to resist the temptation of making poor food choices that have the potential of throwing me off track.

Take time today to consider a temptation or secret sin that you have been struggling with in your journey to wellness. Write it down and pray about sharing it with a group member or friend.

____

____

____

Inner Reflection: Do I ask God to help me take responsibility for my actions and then thank Him for providing me a way out when I am tempted? Do I realize He has given me the power, made provisions, and provides peace when I am struggling to make the right choices?

DAY 2 ~ DESIRE CONCEIVED

If we want to overcome temptation, we must at some point put out of our hearts and minds all shifting of blame, especially blaming God. When we understand where temptation really comes from, we begin to rely on God's strength to overcome the power temptation has over us.

Let's read James 1: 13-15.

In verse 14, where does James say temptation comes from?

____

Temptation comes from our own sinful desires. It's a hard fact to accept, but if you and I want to have victory over temptation, we must first acknowledge and be on guard against the lust that resides in our very own body.

The word *lust* means desire and sometimes refers to legitimate desires.

Look up the following Scriptures:

Luke 22:15

Philippians 1:23

1 Thessalonians 2:17

Sometimes the same basic desire may be either legitimate or sinful, depending on the situation and how we handle it.

For example, hunger is a legitimate desire. It is an indicator that our body needs fuel. When we eat to fuel our body using food in the proper way, it is a natural and healthy process. But when we allow food to become the fix for some emotional turmoil we are experiencing or when we eat out of stress, anxiety, or boredom instead of turning to God, then we have allowed the legitimate desire for food to become sin.

Be aware—our own sinful desire lures us away and sin always begins in our minds.

Now here is the page turner for us. To overcome temptation, we must acknowledge that the initial thought to sin is birthed in our mind. It is not sin unless I pursue it or act upon it.

Let's make it our habit to take every thought captive to the obedience of Christ.

Read 2 Corinthians 10:5 and ask the Lord to reveal thoughts we should take captive.

____

____

____

We differ from person to person with regard to the things that tempt us. Why not take a moment and jot down a couple of things that you are now aware of that have been areas of struggle for you over the last few weeks with regard to temptation.

____

____

____

You may want to share these in your group, with one of your leaders, or with a trusted friend. Have someone pray for and with you over these areas of temptation. Make notes this week in your journal each time you have victory in these particular areas.

> ***Inner Reflection: Am I allowing my relationship with God to grow? Am I giving Him permission to help me overcome the unhealthy desires in my life?***

DAY 3 ~ LISTENING AND DOING

Follow-through. I have always struggled with follow-through. During my weight-loss journey I would start the day off right, then life would get me off track. By the end of the day, I had gotten in a hurry or made poor choices. At times I would just get angry at myself. I would throw in the towel before the day was done and say, "Oh well, I will start again tomorrow." Sound familiar? In my mind I knew what I needed to do, but I just struggled to follow through consistently. That same struggle happens in all aspects of our life-change process, and it also happened in the Bible. Take a look at James 1: 19-24.

In verse 20, James points out that the anger of man does not bring about the righteousness of God. Then, in verse 21, he shares with us that in humility we should receive the Word implanted.

In a direct way, James is telling us that anger doesn't work for us or with us, but against the plan that the Lord has for us to accomplish.

Being angry with myself over my weight caused me to hurt others, including members of my own dear family. Anger caused me to abuse myself with food and others with my words. All this worked against the plan the Lord had for me, but as I began to surrender daily in humility to the Lord's plan, follow-through stopped being such a struggle. Praying daily, "Lord, I am not able, but you are through me" gave me the ability to depend on Christ for living in a new place of freedom.

James moves on in verse 22 and places real value on listening much and talking little. He admonishes us not to merely ___________ to the Word but ______ what it says.

Is there an area in your life where you struggle with anger?

____

____

Do you struggle with listening to God?

Explain: ____

____

Are you consistent with doing what He tells you to do?

____

____

Give one example of a change you desire to make. What is one thing you can do to make it happen?

____

____

We can measure the effectiveness of our Bible study time by the effect it has on our behavior and attitudes.

Read Jeremiah 29:11.

What does this verse say the Lord has for us?

____

The Bible says the Lord has good plans for us. They are plans for good and not for disaster, to give us a future and a hope.

Even in our most difficult struggles in the area of bondage, God is there. As we begin to hear the truth of His voice and act upon those changes, the good plans God has for us can be perfected in our lives.

As we become more like Jesus, the reflection in the mirror changes. Slowly we will begin to see the beautiful image of Christ reflected back to us. The reflection of Christ brings joy into a believer's heart.

> *Inner Reflection: God has good plans for me, and if I ask Him to guide me to be slow to speak, to listen carefully, and to rein in my anger with myself and others, He will do it. Do I really believe this?*

DAY 4 ~ PERFECT LAW

Today, let's start by reading James 1: 22-25.

James makes a statement in verse 25 about the perfect law. What does he say it gives us?

____

What is the perfect law for us as believers? _______________________________

It may seem contradictory that a law can give us freedom, but if we take it at face value we can see God's law points out sin in our lives and then gives us the opportunity to ask for forgiveness. God's desire has always been to draw us to Him, and His love and grace frees us from the control that sin once had over us.

He also goes on to say that not forgetting what he has __________, but doing it—he will be __________________ in what He does.

When I first began my weight-loss journey, I struggled with the issue of legalism and love. Here is a good example: when I began to learn about making better food choices, I wanted to know how many French fries I could eat and still be legal. The thought of maybe I just needed to give up eating French fries for a season never entered my mind. Many times I would legally count out those fries, only to default to my past behavior and eat them all. I knew in my mind this was not a wise decision.

Satan was thrilled to see me struggle with legalism. Time and time again he would remind me that it was useless to try to make healthy changes because I would be a failure. He would remind me of all those French fries I was eating. I desired freedom, but my past of trying to do everything perfect and then failing haunted me.

Through the study of God's Word, the Lord began to change every aspect of my journey—instead of trying to be legal, I began to hear the truth and act on it. I started changing my mind about food and fitness, and my body followed the change. I began making changes based on my new desire to be more like Jesus, and it changed everything. God began to change me from the inside out—because of my new love relationship with Him. Now I didn't care how many French fries I could eat. I found freedom in saying, "I don't want that anymore." I realized that tracking my food consistently allowed me the freedom of choosing anything in moderation.

The process of love and obedience in the small things allowed me to see freedom from the weight I had carried for so long. I also found freedom from the legalism that had me bound in a religion instead of a relationship.

Are there places in your wellness journey where you have been trying to do everything perfectly?

____

____

____

The perfect law allows us to obey God because of love. We are then able to walk in obedience, and through this we become believers in action. That is when we are able to find delight and joy in a relationship, not a religion.

Consider writing a prayer of surrender to the Lord today in this area where you have been trying to do everything perfectly. Take some time to journal this week about any changes He makes in your heart as He transforms your actions in this area.

____

____

____

Inner Reflection: In what areas of my life do I need to surrender daily to Christ?

DAY 5 ~ REIGN IN THE TONGUE

As we wrap up the first chapter of James in our study, I want to spend a little time in the last few verses by reading James 1: 26-27.

What does James tell us we need to keep on our tongue?

____

Have you given much consideration to your tongue as far as your speech is concerned? The Bible has a great deal to say on the subject. Look up these verses and jot down in your own words what they mean.

Proverbs 10:19:

____

____

Proverbs 10:32:

____

____

Proverbs 12:18:

____

____

Proverbs 13:3:

____

____

This week, we have studied the value of relying on God's power and strength. We need to continually remind ourselves that the Holy Spirit living in us will give us the power and strength to monitor and control what we say.

Think about a time someone else's words hurt or offended you. How did you react?

____

____

Now think about a time you offended someone else with your words. How did they react and/or how did you respond?

____

____

____

Now give some examples of how our words can encourage others.

____

____

What we say and don't say are both equally important. Remember that the power of life and death resides in our tongue. The only way to be in control is to allow the Holy Spirit to control the tongue.

> **_Inner Reflection: I am beginning to see how powerful my words can be. Am I speaking words of life to those around me...or words of death?_**

DAY 6 ~ STOP AND CONSIDER

Kate Larsen is a health coach, and in her book *Progress not Perfection*[1], she shares about one of the secrets to lasting change. She developed a healthy eating model called (TCAW): Think, Choose, Act, and Win. Kate advocates that real change happens when accompanied by an attitude shift. Simply put, you need an attitude shift that gives you the mental strength and fortitude to resist temptation and stand strong in your resolve to change. Unless we develop that attitude shift Kate talks about, we will continually give into the temptation. So today, take some time to think about an area where you may need to implement this model. Write out your thoughts in the space provided below.

Identify an area in your wellness journey that you really struggle with:

____

____

Think about what needs to change for you to be successful:

____

Choose an alternative plan to help you be successful in making this change:

____

How will you act on these changes today? _______________________________

Win! And when you do, jot down that area of success and thank the Lord for His provision in this area. ____

This same model can be used and implemented with our exercise plan. We cannot wait until we feel like exercising—we must act our way into a new way of feeling. If we wait until we feel like it, we will never begin exercising. Think about the positive reason to implement an exercise plan. Choose a beginning regimen. Do it! Just do it! Act on your choice; don't wait for the feeling. Be consistent, and in the end the feeling will come…Win in the area of exercise.

____

____

____

If we implement change in only one area of our life, we are still in an unbalanced lifestyle. Think about small ways you can implement changes in your mind, body, and life. Write them down in the space provided and pray over the needed changes. God will give you the strength to accomplish all He calls you to do.

____

____

____

[1] Progress not Perfection: Your Journey Matters by Kate Larsen

Expert Publisher (January 1, 2007)

CHOOSE YOUR CHALLENGE FOR THE WEEK

Nutrition Challenge—Goal: Change Your Mind!

1. Avoid fad diets. There are many great eating plans out there. The key is to find the right one for you and then stick with it consistently. Eat sensibly every day and get a healthy balance of fruits and vegetables.
2. Limit fats and high-fat foods, sugar, soft drinks, and candy. Keep sliced vegetables in the fridge in ice water for convenient snacks or for quick-fix recipes at dinner. Steamed or grilled veggies make a great dinner side for fish or shrimp!

Fitness Challenge—Goal: Change Your Body!

1. Write your fitness time in your planner or on your calendar as an appointment with yourself in advance. Then develop and write out an exercise strategy that you can commit to and stick with.
2. When walking this week, bump up the time to 20 minutes. Remember to breathe! Breathing in for four steps and out for two steps is recommended. By the way, move your arms while walking to maximize your workout! Just a little upper body movement makes a whole lot of difference.

Lifestyle Challenge—Goal: Change Your Life!

1. Studies find that friendships are wonderful antidotes to stress. Spend some time this week with a friend. Make a date for lunch, take a walk together, or meet for a game of tennis. Maybe you need to seek out a new friend or renew an old friendship this week. Buddy up with a workout partner…just make sure you buddy up with a pal you can count on to push you and help you reach your goals—not one that will be your partner in the crime of not following through!

CHALLENGE I CHOSE ~ PROGRESS I MADE:

DAY 7 ~ JOURNAL PROMPT:

I want only pure thoughts taking residence in my mind, but when impure thoughts find their way in I know where they come from…

WEEK 3
MERCY TRIUMPHS

Scripture Focus of the Week

Judgment without mercy will be shown to anyone who has not been merciful. Mercy triumphs over judgment.

[James 2:13]

My grandmother sang a song when she was washing clothes on her old ringer washing machine. I don't remember all the words, but she would sing this phrase many times over: "Your grace and mercy have brought me through, I am living this moment because of you." Looking back at the hard life my Little Granny lived, I often wonder how grace and mercy brought her through. If you looked at her circumstances intently, you would have to acknowledge how hard and difficult her life really was. She raised a family of ten during the depression. I would have needed a great deal of mercy and grace just to get through washing the clothes for that many people. Yet Little Granny was not only a joyful person, she was also a thankful person.

We have a tendency to lump grace and mercy together, but they are not the same. How do we know the difference? When is it mercy and when is it grace? Grace is God blessing us despite the fact that we do not deserve it, while mercy is God not punishing us as our sins deserve. Mercy is deliverance from judgment. Grace is extending kindness. As we dive into week three, let's explore how mercy can be the bearer of joy in our lives and what that might look like in our journey toward a life of freedom and balance.

DAY 1 ~ MERCY ACCEPTED

Today let's start our study time by reading James 2:1-13 to give us an overview for the week.

Focus in on verses 12 and 13. What do they say?

[12] _________ and _________ as those who are going to be judged by the law that gives freedom [13] because ______________ without mercy will be shown to anyone who has not been merciful. ____________ triumphs over judgment.

Judgment without mercy will be shown to anyone who has not been merciful. I want to zero in on that thought for a moment. Think about whom we most often judge the hardest. Ourselves.

We judge ourselves many times with no mercy. So often we get caught up in the lie that we are worthless…that making lifestyle changes or improving our health are good ideas but just not possible for us to accomplish. Yet God's mercy defeats all that through the blood of Jesus, who came to destroy the works of the evil one.

Think about some areas in your life where you have shown no mercy to yourself. Ask the Lord to reveal these to you.

____

____

____

One area in my life was when I would make a poor food choice early in the day. I would in most cases throw in the towel for the day…and sometimes for the rest of the week. I would beat myself up with negative self-talk. No mercy!

Now, with the Lord's help, I pray, ask for forgiveness, and then do the next right thing. I extend mercy to myself, and doing so has allowed me to be much more successful in my weight-loss journey.

God's mercy triumphs over our judgment of ourselves, and it starts by accepting the mercy that God has extended even to us.

Inner Reflection: Am I modeling Christ by extending mercy?

DAY 2 ~ MERCY GIVEN

Today let's look at James 2:13 from the New Living Translation:

"There will be no mercy for those who have not shown mercy to others. But if you have been merciful, God will be merciful when he judges you."

Yesterday we talked about how we struggle to extend mercy to ourselves many times. Today we want to go one step further and talk about giving mercy to others.

Keep in mind the definition of mercy. What did we say mercy is?

____

____

Why do we need to show mercy to others?

____

What are some ways you have shown mercy to others?

____

____

What are some ways that others have shown mercy to you?

____

____

God does not want us to be controlled by or held captive to the judgment of others. Instead, we are to fear God who made us and walks with us, and we are to give mercy to others as He does for us. The followers of Jesus are to welcome those bound by the chains of addiction, hardship, and pain. God came to love and to set free everyone who would turn and follow Him.

We, as Jesus followers, are to be known by our love and compassion for everyone no matter how rich, poor, sick, or healthy they are.

Take time to read John 15:12.

"My command is this: Love _________ another as I have loved you."

In light of our study today, consider the name of anyone you have withheld mercy from.

____

____

Ask the Lord to guide you in showing mercy in this situation.

> **Inner Reflection: Have I thanked Jesus for the mercy He has given me? Have I asked Him to help me give others that same mercy, love, and compassion?**

DAY 3 ~ MERCY SHOWN

Let's start our study time today by re-reading James 2:1-13 so we can dig another layer deeper into mercy.

James argues against favoritism of any sort. If we look past the surface of this Scripture, I believe James is painting a beautiful picture that draws us into God's view. We are all equal. The ground at the foot of the cross is level on all sides. God's mercy is shown to us all at the same price. That fact is so important because as followers of Jesus we are no longer bound by the lies of Satan or the chains of darkness.

Write out what Ephesians 5:8 says:

____

____

We "were full of darkness" but now we have "light from the Lord". Sin and evil no longer have a hold on us.

As believers, we are commanded to obey Christ. The key is staying close to Jesus and listening to His voice instead of relying on rules or boundaries drawn in the proverbial sand. The law is no longer an external set of rules, but the law of liberty, which we now joyfully and willingly carry out. Jesus said that we, as His followers, are to be known for our love for each other…James tells us that we are to "speak and act".

I want you to take a moment and consider your attitude concerning your wellness journey. Are you embracing the changes you are making in your lifestyle? Or do the changes you are making seem restrictive? Be honest and share your feelings below.

____

____

Inner Reflection: As we pursue balance, it will be an ongoing process and difficult at times. Charting our progress is meant to keep us on track as we spend time changing our minds and bodies. At times the changes will seem restrictive, but I am reminded that James points us to speak and act the love of Christ.

DAY 4 ~ REAL FAITH – RIGHT ACTIONS

Let's move on and read James 2:14-17.

Look up the following Scriptures. What is the common thread in each one?

Hebrews 11:1 ____

Hebrews 11:6 ____

Ephesians 2:8 ____

1 Thessalonians 1:2-3 ________________________________

Romans 10:17 ____

What do you believe James is saying about salvation, faith, and works?

____

____

____

____

We cannot earn our salvation by serving and obeying God. Works of loving service are not a substitute for, but rather a verification of, our faith in Christ.

Good works can never earn salvation, but true faith always—let me say it again—always results in a changed life. Good works are then a by-product of that changed life.

When we believe in God, we act on our faith in Him, and this puts feet to our faith because a faith that has no works is not really faith at all.

True faith involves a commitment of your whole self to God. The same is true in our journey to wholeness. Have you fully committed this process to God? Have you surrendered your will and rights in all areas?

Take a moment and fully commit your journey to the Lord's guidance. As we move forward, let's allow our actions to reflect that commitment. Write a prayer reflecting this commitment.

____

____

____

____

Inner Reflection: On days when the desire to quit, give up, and go back to my old ways seem overwhelming, who will I rely on for strength?

DAY 5 ~ ABRAHAM'S FAITH

It helps to look in Scripture and find role models as we journey through life. There are many who experienced difficult days and struggled throughout their lives. If we read and study their lives, we can benefit by seeing how they were still able to count it all joy because of their faith in God.

James used the example of Abraham as a man who received God's promise…not because of works or through his own efforts, but because of his faith.

As you read your lesson today, think about your own faith in God. Consider whether you might receive God's promise because of your genuine faith in a merciful God who loves and cares for you.

Read Galatians 3:6-12.

What was credited to Abraham, and why?

____

____

Who are the real children of Abraham according to verse 7?

____

Look up Genesis 15:6 and write it out here.

____

____

Abraham's faith saved him. That is still true for people today. You can substitute your name for Abraham's when you place your faith in God. What a comfort it is to know we cannot work for our place in Heaven; we need only to place our faith in God and it will be counted to us as righteousness. Have you placed your faith in God? If not, today would be a great time to do so. Once you do, joy and peace will fill your heart.

Dear Jesus, I stand in awe of your amazing love and I [insert your name] want to place my faith in you just like Abraham did. I accept the free gift of salvation from you, and as I continue my wellness journey, I surrender my will over to your plan and purpose.

Inner Reflection: Have I thanked God lately for the gift of salvation that He has extended to me? Do I have a longing to spend time with Him? Studying God's Word to learn His ways and putting them into practice daily will allow my faith to be as strong as Abraham's.

DAY 6 ~ STOP AND CONSIDER

As I reflect back on this week's study on mercy, it sounds like an easy concept…yet in reality, it is difficult. It is difficult to love and forgive others who have hurt us…and then to extend mercy. Extending mercy the way Christ has modeled it for us can only happen by His strength and power within us. Extending mercy seems to be one of the many things that trips us up and slows us down in our wellness journey.

I understand what Paul meant in Hebrews 12:1 when he said to strip off every weight that slows us down or hinders us—especially the sin that so easily trips us up. Holding on to things like doubt, fear, anger, and unforgiveness hinders us in finding real joy. Some of the very things that may be holding you back could be weight that God never meant for you to carry. It may be time to throw it off.

Today, take time to consider what you need to strip off so you can press forward into the next stretch of your journey. What do you need to let go of so that you can renew your energy, self-esteem, and confidence?

____

____

____

I think about all the times I have started strong, made a poor decision, and then felt and acted like a failure on this wellness journey. Let's move past just our weight-loss journey, though. Think about all the times we have said hurtful things to others, told an untruth, or allowed jealousy to rear its head in a relationship. All the things that show up on a daily basis…and then, here is Jesus in the middle of the mess. He steps in and extends the mercy we so desperately need but feel unworthy of. The truth is, we are not worthy and never will be. Jesus extends the mercy and grace we so desperately long for, and because of His great love for us we can become more like Him.

Let's think about our desires and actions for a moment. Are we willing to sacrifice our desires until we no longer want to go back to an unhealthy lifestyle? Developing a daily dependence on Christ will be the key that can unlock the door to real and lasting change.

Take time to write a prayer of surrender to the Lord in your journal, asking Him to give you a desire to love Him first. Then throw off everything that is hindering your success, asking Him to help you run with endurance to the finish.

CHOOSE YOUR CHALLENGE FOR THE WEEK

NUTRITION CHALLENGE—GOAL: CHANGE YOUR MIND!

1. Add fruit to your morning cereal or add in a piece at lunch/afternoon snack.
2. Have some fruit for dessert after dinner, or try grilling fresh fruit on the grill. (It is awesome!!)
3. See how many different kinds of fruit you can eat this week. Try a different kind every day.

FITNESS CHALLENGE—GOAL: CHANGE YOUR BODY!

1. Before you walk, march in place for a few minutes to warm up your muscles. Swing your arms in wide movements over your head, then add a few leg lifts. As you walk this week, walk at a little faster pace than last week. Remember to swing your arms to add in the upper body workout! Push a little harder than last week. Come on, you can do it!
2. Keep looking for ways to add more movement to your daily life: walking to errands instead of driving, taking the stairs, getting up to change the channel, deliberately parking further from the store entrance, etc.

LIFESTYLE CHALLENGE—GOAL: CHANGE YOUR LIFE!

1. If you are the type who is always too busy, list all of your activities, chores, and commitments. Then divide them into three categories: those you must do, those you love to do, and those you do because you think you should. This week, eliminate one item from the "because you think you should list" and schedule one fun activity. No TV, though! Notice I said an activity you enjoy. Have some fun…plan it and then do it!

CHALLENGE I CHOSE ~ PROGRESS I MADE:

DAY 7 ~ JOURNAL PROMPT

How many times have I failed to show mercy to myself? If God shows me mercy (and He does), should I not do the same?

WEEK 4
JOYFUL FAITH THAT WORKS

Scripture Focus of the Week

As the body without the spirit is dead, so faith without deeds is dead.

[James 2:26]

A beautiful thing happened early in my weight-loss journey: the Lord sent an awesome group of friends willing to get in the trenches and help me make progress. They not only came along side and encouraged me, they modeled what healthy should and could look like. They never pushed me to be like them; rather, they continually pointed me to follow the course the Lord was laying out for me. What I could not do on my own for so many years happened when the Lord paired me up with the right team. My life and weight-loss journey began to change for the better.

There are some things in this life that just go hand in hand. For instance, peanut butter and jelly, cheese and crackers, salt and pepper, up and down…just to name a few. Preparing and planning are kind of like that, and so are food and exercise. One supports the other. Doing one without the other may allow us to see short-term results, but if long-term, life-changing results are the goal, we need properly balanced combinations.

This week, let's focus our attention on another balanced combination: faith and works. James presents a clear understanding that a real joy-filled faith is not a belief in works but a belief that works. These works are produced out of a settled faith and trust in God. Let's see how this pair goes hand in hand.

DAY 1 ~ JOYFUL TRUST

Let's begin out study time this week by reading James 2:14-26.

Write out James 2:26:

As the _________ without the __________ is dead, so _________ without _________ is dead

What connection does James make between faith and deeds?

____

____

____

James' plural use of the word **work** throughout the passage is an indication that our work or works should be a continual process. James is clear: works are the evidence of a real faith. There can be no good works unless there is already faith (trust) in God.

James isn't implying we should work for the benefit of others that are in need of faith in Christ. He is showing us that Christians will have works for the benefit of others in need as a result of placing their faith in Christ. When we love Jesus, we cannot help but love and care for others.

Let's finish today by looking up John 14:12.

Who is speaking in this verse? _______________________________

Jesus tells us that whoever believes in Him will do the works He has been doing…and they will do even greater things than these.

Close your time in study today by listing ways you can reach out to someone in need. Who can you love this week?

____

____

____

____

Sometimes it is difficult to know what others might need help with, so take a moment and write out a simple prayer to help you get started.

____

____

____

Here is an example of the one I use: Dear Jesus, make me faithful in all that I think, say, and do. I ask You to protect me from being spiritually dead in my faith. Show me ways that I can love others as You love me.

> ***Inner Reflection: Have I made time this week to connect with others and pray for friends helping me in my journey?***

DAY 2 ~ REHAB'S RIGHTOUSNESS

Today let's re-read James 2:14-26.

Verse 25 talks about Rahab the harlot who lived in Jericho. When Israel's spies came to the city, she hid them and helped them escape. In this way, she demonstrated faith in God's purpose for Israel. Rahab's faith and conviction in God gave her the courage she needed to demonstrate her faith.

Like Rahab, what we believe should be demonstrated in the way we act. What are some ways that we can demonstrate our faith?

____

____

____

Now take a moment to think of some ways you can demonstrate (or some ways you are demonstrating) your new lifestyle? Jot them down here.

____

____

____

____

Read Romans 4:1-5.

What does the passage say their faith is credited as? _______________________

What is righteousness?

____

Righteousness is defined as "the quality of being morally correct and justifiable".

How can we use Rahab's faith and her actions and as an example to apply to our lives?

____

____

She did not wait until the spies were in her town and in her home to stake her faith in the Lord. She was already grounded in her belief. Her heart had already been changed. As a result, the decision to help the spies was an easy choice. She did the right thing.

Inner Reflection: Have I staked my faith in Christ and Christ alone? Do I trust Christ to guide me completely and without reservation? Do I love Him more than food?

DAY 3 ~ JOY IN SALVATION

Let's take time and look up the following Scriptures:

Luke 19:10 ____

John 3:16 ____

Mark 10:45 ____

John 6:51 ____

When we look in Scripture and examine heroes of the faith like Abraham and Rahab, we have to ask what made them different. Was it just a belief? Head knowledge? Or is there something more?

A transformed life, like that experienced by Abraham and Rahab, is there for us if we follow the apostle Peter's instruction: "Repent, and let every one of you be baptized in the name of Jesus Christ for the remission of sins; and you shall receive the gift of the Holy Spirit" (Acts 2:38).

A prayer of repentance is the first step in the right direction to life change. *Real* life change.

Praying such a prayer does not have to be complicated or lengthy, just simply from the heart and to the point. Here is an example: Dear Heavenly Father, I acknowledge You as Lord of my life. Forgive me for my sin. I ask You to come into my heart today and be Lord of my life. Change me from the inside out so I may honor You in all I do. Amen.

Have you taken that first step? If so, please share here.

____

____

____

Inner Reflection: I do not need to be afraid of sharing the truth that has set me free from the bondage of sin. Who does God want me to share it with?

DAY 4 ~ IS FAITH ENOUGH?

Read and write out James 2:14.

____

____

____

What does James question here concerning faith by itself not being accompanied by action?

____

____

James wants us to really consider the parallel of what we say and what we do. True faith transforms our conduct as well as our thoughts.

Write out James 2:17 below and circle the word **dead**.

____

____

James wants us to know we cannot earn our salvation by serving and obeying God, but those actions reveal our commitment to God is real. The works that James directs us to here are simply a verification of our faith in Christ.

Let's finish by reading and writing out James 2:18.

____

____

____

At a glance, this verse seems contradictory, but deeper investigation clarifies for us that our good works can never earn salvation; true faith always results in a changed life, and good works will naturally follow.

Faith, placed in the Lord Jesus Christ, is enough. Some people try to add to it saying there must be more. There is no substitution for faith that brings us salvation.

Nothing we do will earn us salvation. James 2:24 says, "You see that a person is considered righteous by what they do and not by faith alone." The passage in James 2:14-26 that we studied previously is about proving the authenticity of your faith by what you do. If your faith in Jesus Christ is real, it will result in good works. In other words, your works demonstrate, and are proof of, your faith. Salvation is by faith alone. We demonstrate our faith in Jesus Christ by what we do.

This subject of faith being enough reminds me of how dependent I am on God to help me in my wellness journey. I cannot do this on my own, but I must have the faith and believe that by His power I can be successful at making long-term change. Staking my faith in Christ alone equips me to make the necessary changes, no matter how difficult.

If you struggle with making long-term changes in your wellness journey, spend some time today reflecting on a couple of changes you really need to make so that you can be more successful.

Commit the list to prayer on a daily basis over the coming weeks. Write each change into a statement that starts like this:

Dear Lord, I have faith in you and believe you want to change how much I eat. Help me measure my portions on all my food choices.

Dear Lord, I have faith in you and believe you want to change:

____

Help me to:

____

____

Dear Lord, I have faith in you and believe you want to change:

____

Help me to:

____

____

Inner Reflection: Do my actions reflect that my commitment to God is real?

DAY 5 ~ TWO TYPES OF FAITH

Yesterday, we studied real faith and learned that it alone brings salvation. But might there be another type of faith we need to learn about? If someone claims to have faith, it may be they are abiding by a set of Christian teachings. They may have an intellectual agreement. The two types of faith are true faith and incomplete faith.

How would you define true faith? (Look at Hebrews 11:1 for help, or review yesterday's lesson.)

____

____

How would you describe incomplete faith?

____

____

If you described incomplete faith as "faith without action", you're on the right track. Agreement with a set of Christian teachings in place of faith in the Lord Jesus Christ is incomplete. True faith will transform our actions and how we think. True faith means your actions will prove your faith.

With Jesus' help, we are able to demonstrate our faith through our actions. It is also reflected in how we treat others.

Do you know which kind of faith you have? Explain.

____

____

Building a foundation of faith started for me when I was twelve years old, sitting in the back pew at Highland Baptist Church. The message that Sunday night spoke to me, and in that moment I knew I had no hope. I knew about Jesus (head knowledge), but I did not know Jesus (heart knowledge). I practically ran up the aisle, and I asked Jesus to come into my heart and forgive me for all my sin. My life changed that night, but I don't think at the age of twelve I really understood the radical impact Jesus wanted to have on my whole person. I had my "life insurance", but it was a term policy, not a whole-life policy at that point.

At age thirty, I cashed in that "term" policy with the Lord and bought into the "whole life" concept. At twelve, I had made Him my Savior, but at thirty, I surrendered all and made Him Lord in every area of my life. That is the same faith of Abraham and Rahab that we have studied this week.

Jesus changed my whole person because I allowed Him to have control. The key to change came when I took that first step and realized Jesus did not want to be part of my life. He wanted to *be* my life.

If there is any doubt concerning the type of faith you have, ask the Lord to give you the courage to talk to someone about how you can receive real faith.

Inner Reflection: What have I done this week to show I have true faith?

DAY 6 ~ STOP AND CONSIDER

As I was writing this book, a precious friend stepped from this life into eternity. We have a tendency to put off eternal decisions. Susan, however, placed her faith in God long ago. She chose to have faith in the one true God. It was an intellectual decision that blossomed into a transforming, genuine faith. Her faith gave her the foundation and anchor she needed when the storm of cancer came crashing upon her at the very young age of fifty-four.

Her anchor was set in the Rock that would not be moved. Just as Abraham set his face toward the mountain, so did Susan. Her intellectual decision of faith made room for a transforming work in her heart, allowing her to gain an eternal perspective. She lived life to the fullest because she began to live intentionally while focusing eternally. People were loved and lives were changed because of the joy which overflowed from Susan's life.

Until the end, she allowed joy to be the fruit of her spirit. Then, as she stepped from this life into the arms of Jesus, her joy became indestructible—a perfect body with a perfect Savior. As difficult as it was for my heart to let Susan go, I know that even though I touched her hand and her sweet face for the last time here on this earth, I will see her again in Heaven. Faith gives me that assurance. I told Susan I would see her later, and she looked up into my face with that same solid faith. She set her eyes toward the mountain.

Is there someone in your life that has exhibited great faith? How did that make you feel?

____

____

____

Share your experience with your group this week.

Inner Reflection: Lord, do I have the assurance in my heart that because I know You as my Savior, when I step out of this life into the next You will be holding my hand?

CHOOSE YOUR CHALLENGE FOR THE WEEK

NUTRITION CHALLENGE—GOAL: CHANGE YOUR MIND!

1. Hit Subway for lunch and order a veggie or turkey sub (make sure you ask for the wheat bread), or try Chick-Fil-A and order the grilled chicken sandwich on the wheat bun with a fruit cup instead of those fries.
2. Complement your healthy meal of steamed veggies and grilled chicken this week by adding brown rice.
3. Add oatmeal to your breakfast plan, or try some whole wheat waffles or pancakes topped with yogurt and fresh fruit.

FITNESS CHALLENGE—GOAL: CHANGE YOUR BODY!

1. It may be time for you to add some tennis, swimming, volleyball, golf, bowling, or bike riding to your fitness plan. The more types of activity you add, the more enjoyable your fitness program will become.
2. Start adding some simple balancing exercises to your routine. A single-leg stance is challenging but a great place to start. Here's how you do this one: stand behind a steady, solid chair (not one with wheels), and hold on to the back of it. Lift up your right foot and balance on your left foot. Hold that position for as long as you can, then switch feet. The goal should be to stand on one foot (without holding onto the chair) for up to a minute.

LIFESTYLE CHALLENGE—GOAL: CHANGE YOUR LIFE!

1. Plan a 5-minute break each day to relax. The art of relaxation is as simple as sitting down, closing your eyes, and thinking of nothing but breathing—breathing in and breathing out! STOP! Don't turn that TV on. Just relax! Did you know that a 5-minute relaxation technique is also a great way to start a quiet time? Prepare your mind for time with God this week by taking a moment to relax before you start your quiet time.

CHALLENGE I CHOSE ~ PROGRESS I MADE:

____

____

____

____

____

____

____

____

____

____

____

____

____

____

____

____

____

____

DAY 7 ~ JOURNAL PROMPT

My eternal perspective is…

WEEK 5
JOYFUL SPEECH

Scripture Focus of the Week

But no man can tame the tongue. It is a restless evil, full of deadly poison.

[James 3:8]

There is a little song or chant most of us know and have heard through the years that says, "Sticks and stones may break my bones but words will never hurt me." Words can't break bones, but they sure have the power to break and wound hearts. This week we are going to evaluate our words and the power they possess to bring or give life and death to the body. Words are one of the essential tools that we use to communicate with others. In a world filled with new technology and ways to communicate like texting and social media, the power in our words becomes more obvious than ever.

What does joyful speech look like? How can we use the power of the tongue in our wellness journey to bring life into our behavior patterns? Let's get started by looking at the power the tongue has.

DAY 1 ~ THE TONGUE: SMALL BUT POWERFUL

Let's see just how powerful our words are as we continue our reading in James 3:1-12.

Focus in on James 3:3–4. James uses two common but very visual illustrations here.

What two common objects does he compare the tongue to?

A _____________ in a _______________ mouth and the _____________on a

_________________.

He says the tongue is like the bit in the mouth of a horse. This tiny piece of metal controls the enormous power and energy of the horse and is used to give it direction. Have you ever been to a horse show or seen horses in a parade? Think about the extraordinary power and influence concentrated in one small object. Those big animals were being controlled by that small bit placed within their mouth.

Do you think it is possible to "bridle" the tongue? Why or why not?

____

James also compares the tongue to the rudder in a boat. We know that a large ship can carry many people. Have you ever been on a cruise ship? That large vessel is simply directed by a turn of the rudder!

So it is with our tongue. The tongue is small, but its power, both for good and for evil, is great.

Think of a time when you said something that hurt someone else.

____

Now consider a time that you talked to yourself in a negative or hurtful way.

____

Explain how you felt. ____

____

Read Matthew 12:34. Where does this verse say our words come from?

____

The Bible says the mouth speaks what the heart is full of. Another translation says out of the abundance of the heart the mouth speaks.

Have you ever wondered why the doctor asks us to stick out our tongue? Doctors can tell a great deal about our health in just the inspection of our tongues.

Controlling our tongue has both negative and positive aspects. It involves the ability to restrain the tongue in silence. But it also means being able to control it in gracious speech when required.

In closing today, write out Proverbs 4:23.

____

____

____

Inner Reflection: Has my tongue been an instrument of healing or hurt?

DAY 2 ~ THE TONGUE: IGNITING SPARKS

In June 2002, a fire known as the Hayman Fire destroyed more than 137,000 acres of mountain forest in Colorado. Cites some forty miles away were said to be affected by the smoke, and thousands of people had to evacuate their homes. Millions of dollars were spent fighting the destructive blaze that began with a single match. Loss of life occurred directly and indirectly while the fire burned from June 8th until July 18th, when it was classified as contained.

Look up James 3:5-6. How does James describe the damage done by our careless and hurtful words?

____

____

We underestimate the destructive power our words can have. As an overweight teenager, I became the brunt of many jokes and much ridicule in and out of school because of my size. Hurtful words cut deep and left scars that have taken many years to heal. Many times throughout my life, I have turned to food for comfort from harsh words and hurtful remarks.

How about you? Have there been times that you have used food or some other substance to medicate due to someone's hurtful words?

____

Think of a time when you allowed a sharp word, a callous remark, or a negative thought to spark that inferno of emotional harm. How did you react?

____

List some ways which may help you avoid saying hurtful or damaging words to others. (Example: Resolve to always say words that are kind about others, ask God to hold your tongue, or choose to say nothing at all.)

____

____

____

Look up the following Scriptures: What do they all have in common about our words?

Proverbs 15:1   ____

Proverbs 15:4   ____

Proverbs 18:4   ____

This week, take some time to evaluate your words, first to others and then to yourself. Negative self-talk is a very powerful and a destructive form of words.

Ask the Lord to guide you to the kind of words you have been using:

1. A fiery blaze as destructive as a blazing fire
2. A life-giving water that brings refreshing joy to the soul

Share your answer here:

Consider how your words may be hindering your wellness journey. Write your thoughts below to share with a friend or in your Bible study group.

Inner Reflection: How do the words I speak to myself help or hinder me?

DAY 3 ~ THE TONGUE: UNDER CONTROL

Write out James 3:8, this week's Scripture focus.

____

____

Looking at this verse can be kind of depressing. James is very clear that none of us have the ability in our own strength to tame our tongue. So why try?

But there is hope! The Bible tells us that with the help of the Holy Spirit we can have power to tame our tongue. Read the following Bible verses:

Colossians 4:6

Ephesians 4:29

Proverbs 10:19

Proverbs 15:4

Now, look up Proverbs 4:23-24.

The exhortation of Proverbs to "keep your heart with all vigilance" is immediately followed by an exhortation to "put away from you crooked speech, and put devious talk far from you".

Sin may find its easiest exit route from our hearts via the mouth. Guarding the heart involves guarding the tongue. Our tongues can be the most difficult thing to control and leave us with great regret if we use our words to hurt.

Consider if there might be someone that you have hurt with your words. Ask the Holy Spirit to reveal this to you. (There could be several people.)

____

____

____

____

____

Whether you intentionally or unintentionally hurt someone with your words, ask the Lord for forgiveness. Then pray and ask the Lord's guidance in talking with that person and asking for forgiveness for the careless words that were spoken.

Taming our tongue is really impossible in our own strength. To find healing from careless words spoken to us is also difficult to overcome. We need the Holy Spirit to be active and present in our lives because by the strength of the Holy Spirit all things are possible.

Write out Philippians 4:13 in the space below.

____

____

You may also want to write it on an index card or sticky note and place it on your mirror, refrigerator, or desk at work. This way, every day you can stay focused on the source of your strength.

Inner Reflection: What do I consider unwholesome talk?

DAY 4 ~ THE TONGUE: SPEAKING LIFE OR DEATH

When I was eight years old, my second-grade spelling teacher made a tremendous impact on my life. I remember standing in the hallway after a spelling test, waiting for my punishment: licks on my hands with a ruler. Yes, we got licks for not spelling words correctly. Even as she administered those licks, she praised me for all the words I got right. At one point, she looked me in the eye and told me she believed I could do better. Those words had power and brought joy to my ears and heart.

Just as the right words can bring life and be life-giving, words used incorrectly can bring death to an individual's spirit. Words can mean the difference between being misunderstood and being clear in your communication.

Even in a difficult place, administering licks for misspelled words, my teacher was speaking life-giving words. Did it make a difference? Absolutely! I never missed another spelling word in second grade, and I believe the main reason was that, after every test, my teacher always told me how proud she was of me. Those words were honey to a child's heart.

James wants to clearly guide us. In James 3:9-10, he shows us there is power in our words. Look closely at these two verses.

"9 With the ___________ we ___________ our Lord and Father, and with it we ___________ human beings, who have been made in God's likeness. 10 Out of the same ___________ come ___________ and ___________. My brothers and sisters, this should not be."

As a young child, I experienced the power of positive words in my life; as an overweight teenager, I experienced the crushing hurt of negatively spoken words; and as an adult, I cannot tell you how many times I have let food have power in my life. I have berated myself with negative self-talk over my lack of self-control. I have encouraged and used my words to give strength to others, and at the same time have spoken words in anger, without even thinking. I have hurt myself and others with my words.

Desiring a real heart change, I am resolved to allow the Lord real control in my life in this area. I have set up some practical ways to allow for my words to bring life and healing. Take some time today to look at this model of some practical ways we can use words to bless others as well as ourselves.

1. Pray daily and ask God to give me an awareness and conviction of my words.
2. Practice speaking daily words to myself and to others that are uplifting, encouraging, inspiring, and edifying.
3. Plan out daily, practical ways of blessing others.

Do you notice the common thread? The key is doing things daily. The same is true with doing our Bible study, eating healthy, exercising, and even setting up practical ways to use our words. It has to be *daily*. When these tasks are completed daily, we find we are better equipped to allow the Holy Spirit to be in control of all areas of our life.

Finish today by writing out some practical ways you might bless others this week. (Example: Write a note for your accountability partner this week, send or give your Bible teacher a thank you note for all their hard work in leading class, verbally thank a co-worker for their hard work and commitment on a project, thank a waiter/waitress for their service to you during your lunch or dinner outing.)

____

____

____

____

If you think of other practical ways of blessing others with your words, share them in your group or with your accountability partner.

Inner Reflection: How can I bless myself through words I speak today?

DAY 5 ~THE TONGUE: DOUBLE-TALK

Look at the questions James asks in James 3:11-12.

Just like the pushmi-pullyu, our tongues are constantly in contradiction.

There is a common thread through the book of James. In chapter one, we talked about being double-minded; in chapter two, we looked at how we try to separate faith and works. Here in chapter three, James pounds out a clear message on double-talk.

The tongue is not just personally destructive, but also damaging to our relationships. How have you personally experienced this?

____

____

Has there been a time lately when you have lashed out with your tongue?

____

____

Look up Matthew 7:18-20, then Matthew 15:18.

Things we say to ourselves can certainly defile us. We tell ourselves and others things like, "I'm getting serious about making some healthy lifestyle changes or losing some weight", but our actions prove it to be double-talk. Our actions must match our talk. Joy comes when we say what we mean and mean what we say.

Think of ways that your actions do not match your talk…be honest.

____

____

Now consider some actions you can take to bring your talk and walk into unity.

____

____

Inner Reflection: Where did the root of unhealthy words start for me?

DAY 6 ~ STOP AND CONSIDER

As we have studied chapter three in the book of James, we have been given a variety of examples about the tongue. James begins verse one with a wise word of caution to those who aspire to be teachers. He also comments in verse two about none of us being perfect. James continually points to the truth and wisdom that we are responsible for our words. Even if we are not leaders of a group or class, we still hold positions of authority. What we say is a direct reflection of our maturity.

James is clear that what comes out of the mouth is a direct overflow of what we hold in our hearts.

What are the descriptions and the dangers of the tongue that we see in James 3:6 & 8?

Description   Danger (warning)

Verse 6:_______________________   _______________________

Verse 8:_______________________   _______________________

Concentrate on ways you can honor God with your speech. Try to make the connection to your wellness journey. I will list some and you finish the list:

1. Confess Jesus as our Lord and Savior

2. Tell others about God's great love for you and for them

3. Speak the truth in love

4. Encourage others in your group or your accountability partner

5. ____

6. ____

7. ____

When I struggled to stay focused through my wellness journey, I found encouragement in coming alongside someone else. God provided me with the words He knew would help others who were also struggling. I believe the spoken word is one of the most powerful tools we have.

When I was a child, my mother was very critical, and things she spoke wounded my spirit. On the other hand, it caused me to be determined to encourage my own children on a daily basis. Finding something positive to say in every situation took practice and persistence on my part. Struggling with my weight for so many years caused me to develop a great deal of destructive and negative self talk that was difficult to overcome. I know from my own personal journey that I speak a great deal more grace into others than I give myself.

Write out a prayer of repentance, a positive affirmation, or a verse that will help you in this very important area of your life.

____

____

____

____

____

Inner Reflection: What thoughts do I need to reign in so that with God's help I can stay in control of my behavior? Do I know by the guidance of the Holy Spirit when to be silent and when to speak?

CHOOSE YOUR CHALLENGE FOR THE WEEK

NUTRITION CHALLENGE—GOAL: CHANGE YOUR MIND!

1. Make a list of your favorite top five high fat/calorie foods (cookies, candy, ice cream, potato chips, etc.). Now gradually downshift. Eliminate these foods from your program by replacing them with a healthier choice. Learn to choose things you like and that are good for you! Remember, this is a process and it will take time.
2. Choose an apple with a tablespoon of peanut butter for a snack this week.
3. Fresh veggies and hummus make a great snack.

FITNESS CHALLENGE—GOAL: CHANGE YOUR BODY!

1. Five days this week, go for a 30-minute walk. Walk at a slightly faster pace than last week and remember to swing your arms to add in the upper body workout. Push a little harder than last week! Come on, you can do it! Stay strong. Remember, as you increase your walking time you may need to support your feet with extra cushioning insoles in your walking shoes.
2. Add some wall push-ups to your strength training. Stand at arm's length in front of a wall that doesn't have any paintings, decorations, windows, or doors. Lean forward slightly and put your palms flat on the wall at the height and width of your shoulders. Keep your feet planted as you slowly bring your body toward the wall. Gently push yourself back so that your arms are straight. Do twenty of these.

LIFESTYLE CHALLENGE GOAL—CHANGE YOUR LIFE!

1. Write down your worries in your prayer journal…be very specific. (Example: I am worried about losing my job.) Ask yourself, "How likely is this to happen?" and "What can I do to be more prepared or put my mind at ease?" Then pray about your concern. Consider volunteering. Helping others lets you put your own problems into perspective and also provides social interaction. Some great places to volunteer: schools, nursing homes, church daycares, and local shelters. As we focus on eliminating unnecessary worry, we find we can be more balanced in our whole person.

CHALLENGE I CHOSE ~ PROGRESS I MADE:

DAY 7 ~ JOURNAL PROMPT

If I gave full control of my tongue over to the Lord, my life would…

WEEK 6
JOYFUL SOWING

Scripture Focus of the Week

Peacemakers who sow in peace raise a harvest of righteousness.

[James 3:18]

Life is filled with many choices. Whether we think about it or not, these choices affect everything we do. The concept of sowing is found throughout the Bible. This week, as we take time to study some of these concepts, I pray they will help us realize how important our choices are. You always reap what you sow—always. Or do you? When I think of the concept of reaping what we sow, I find I usually think of this in the negative sense. I think of paying the consequences for sinful actions or foolish choices. But the laws of the harvest are not just negative, as we will see this week. So be encouraged. These laws are also positive and stand as a promise of blessing for sowing that which is good, peaceable, reasonable, helpful, and healthful.

Throughout my wellness journey, I have sown seeds of life change. The process did not stop at planting, and at times it has been difficult and painful. There have been seasons of cultivating my new lifestyle and studying for a better harvest. Prayer and time have been invested, and through it all, I have found if I am faithful to the sowing process, God is faithful in producing a harvest of change, which brings real and lasting joy to my life. The same thing is possible for you. Are you ready to plant a few seeds this week in your life-change process? Let's dig in and see what happens.

DAY 1 ~ WISDOM REVEALED

Have you ever known anyone who claimed to be wise but acted foolishly? Let's begin our study today by reading James 3:13-18.

For the sake of today's study, let's drill down on verse 13.

According to this verse, how do we show wisdom?

____

____

Just as you can identify a tree by the type of fruit it produces, you can evaluate your wisdom by the way you act. Wisdom, or let's say godly wisdom, will always lead to peace and goodness.

Think about a time you were tempted to escalate some conflict…or maybe you simply fanned flames of discord with a friend or a family member. Briefly share what happened.

____

____

Now think about what the outcome might have looked like if you had given a soft answer or loving words instead.

____

____

Do you consider yourself a peacemaker? Why or why not?

____

____

Read Matthew 5:9. What does it say peacemakers are?

____

Yes, it says peacemakers are blessed. I want to be blessed in my life, and I want to sow the seeds of a peacemaker.

It takes time to grow, change, and overcome the poor habits that are so much a part of our lifestyle—sometimes since childhood. Realize that we can sow into any area of our life, either sparingly or bountifully, whether it is spiritual, relational, financial, emotional, or physical. But we will only get out what we put in.

Let's look at some of the daily habits (seeds) that you have been sowing in your wellness journey over the last few weeks.

____

____

____

Now evaluate your progress and decide if you are reaping the desired harvest of those habits (seeds).

____

____

What habit (seed) needs the most work to achieve the goals and results you're looking for?

____

____

Inner Reflection: How can I practice the principle of seed-sowing in all areas of my life as I seek to be more like Him?

DAY 2 ~ EARTHLY WISDOM

Today, I want us to look at another kind of seed: the seed of earthly wisdom revealed in James 3:14-15.

In verse 14, what does James say we may have in our hearts? _______________ _______________ and _______________ _______________

If we do, James says do not be _______________________________________

It is so easy for us to be drawn into wrong desires by the pressures of society and sometimes well-meaning friends and loved ones. And when we compare ourselves to others, Satan uses that as a seed of destruction to plant jealously in our hearts. Let's guard our hearts above all else, because in Proverbs 4:23 it says:

____

____

Everything we do flows from the heart. If the goal is to plant real life change, where does the seed need to be planted? _______________________

Look up 1 Corinthians 2:6. What does this verse tell us about wisdom?

____

____

____

Just as sowing can produce good things that are the fruit of life, sowing the wrong seeds can produce things that are the fruit of death. Failure is a seed many of us have planted into our hearts, minds, and spirits. I believe that is one of the reasons it's easy to give up.

For us to find freedom and life, this seed cannot be cut off at the ground; it has to be dug up and the root removed. If not, it continues to grow back even among the good seed of truth and life, choking out the good of our new lifestyle.

Can you think of other seeds which may need to be cut off at the ground, dug up, and removed?

Circle the ones below most challenging to you.

Anger	Bitterness	Compulsive Eating	Gossip
Greed	Destructive	Competitiveness	Alcohol Abuse
Gambling	Overspending	Pornography	Unforgiveness

If you have challenges that are not listed, write them here.

____

____

Take some time this week to pray about steps you may need to take to dig up this destructive seed by the root and put it to death so it no longer has a hold on you. This may take some time and prayer. Remember, we cannot change everything at once. Let's replace those seeds of death with seeds of life change. The next few weeks can be a time of planting and replacing. One of the greatest tools we have to move from failure to faith is positive affirmations.

Inner Reflection: What are the affirmations I need most today?

DAY 3 ~ DISCOVERING DISORDERED SOWING

At times, I feel like the little hamster in the pet store running around and around on the metal wheel in his cage…running faster and faster but never making any real progress and ending up spent and exhausted. Making changes in a hit-and-miss order leads me to destructive habits and discouragement. Satan loves the chaos we allow him to create in our lives. It keeps us on the wheel, running faster and faster but never truly seeing real progress and change.

Read James 3:16.

____

____

Now look at Luke 8:7 & 14.

Disordered sowing (seed sown among the thorns) lures us to a life of sin, bondage, worries, and strife. This type of sowing leaves no room in our lives for the good things of God. Applying God's Word helps us sow good seed in good ground. For example, a muscle when exercised will grow stronger and leaner, but the unused muscle will grow weak and flabby.

Disordered sowing may be carried forward from childhood and therefore has had plenty of time to take root and spread. One which was sown into my life was the seed of a critical spirit. My mother had one, and even though she loves the Lord, she allowed her critical spirit to cause much pain in the lives of her children. I believe a great deal of our negative self-talk is a result of people around us who have a critical spirit.

Do a self-evaluation concerning your attitude toward your weight-loss progress and a critical spirit. If you see any connections between the two, write them out in the space below.

____

____

____

____

Have you caught yourself talking negatively to yourself when you don't see progress as you follow your wellness plan? List a few of the things you tell yourself. How can you rephrase them into something positive?

____

____

____

____

____

____

I developed a mindset of learning to speak only that which is pure, lovely, or uplifting. To this day, I make great effort in continuing this process. The world draws us into destructive patterns, but, through the power of Christ, we can be set free.

Inner Reflection: How has God guided me to a life of ordered sowing so that my life will produce an abundant harvest?

DAY 4 ~ LIFE-CHANGING SEED OF HEAVENLY WISDOM

Weight loss is conditional on making physical changes to your diet and exercise plan. Life change is a precious gift from a loving Father who loves us too much to leave us in the condition we are in. He does not force us to make changes, though. He allows us to surrender to His wisdom. As we do, change becomes the natural process.

We all deal with challenges of some sort. If we only focus on the weight, then once it's gone, the other issues will surface. Diets will always put us back where we started, but by planting seeds of real life change, the harvest will bring us to a new place where we become healthy, whole, and free. Our hearts and minds change, and the new spirit in us gives us a desire to never go back to bondage.

Read James 3:17 and describe what heavenly wisdom looks like.

____

____

The characteristics of heavenly wisdom might be called the seeds of peace. The type of wisdom you have, heavenly or earthly, will be revealed in how you act. Choosing heavenly wisdom will enable you to experience real life change. The joy we can experience as we begin choosing God's wisdom more consistently will be evident in our lives.

James presents some characteristics of heavenly wisdom: walking in integrity with God and others (pure); refusing to incite anger in other people (peace-loving); valuing and accepting other people's feelings (considerate); forgiving others' mistakes and sins (merciful); and being transparent about my weaknesses (sincerity).

Read Romans 12:9 and fill in the blank.

Love must be __________________________.

The last characteristic of heavenly wisdom listed in James 3:17 is sincerity. The verse in Romans tells us that love must be sincere. Being insincere is an earthly trait. Think of an example of insincere love in relation to other people. Write out one way to replace that with a sincere love.

____

There may be people in your church or where you work, play, or live who need sincere love in their life. It's easy to pretend to love, care, or listen. We may at times pretend to take an interest in others. God wants us to love with sincerity, have honest compassion, and listen deeply.

When we plant with heavenly wisdom, our lives will change. It will take time, but sincere love requires work and effort. It involves planting into others, helping them become better individuals. In the process of sowing into others with a sincere love, we become a harvest of change, and when a sprout of change breaks forth, we become a better person, beautiful and full of joy.

1 Corinthians 1:30 tells us that Jesus is wisdom from God. Let's use that verse as we close in prayer today.

____

____

____

Inner Reflection: How difficult is it for me to use heavenly wisdom characteristics on a consistent basis?

DAY 5 ~ HARVEST OF RIGHTEOUSNESS

Using God's wisdom, we see that we can plant seeds of trust and obedience, which will bring great peace and joy in our journey to having a changed life. Close your eyes and imagine a field ripe for harvest. The crop you see in the field is righteousness, goodness, and mercy; beautiful fruit that will last and never rot.

How does this happen? The seed for this crop was planted by those who make peace. James elevates the role of those committed to living peacefully in full confidence that God is meeting their every need. Peacemakers do not feel obligated to fight against others for their needs to be met. They simply plant seeds of trust and then rest in the knowledge that God is able to do immeasurably more than we can ask or imagine.

Their lifestyle of trust leads to fields of joyful, righteous living…a changed life. Is it easy? No. Is it possible? Yes. We can do all things through Christ who is our strength.

Read 2 Timothy 2:22.

What are we to pursue? _______________, _____________, ____________, and _____________.

How do we do this? (Hint: first part of verse 22)

____

Just as Timothy was warned to flee anything which might bring on evil thoughts or temptations, we also would be wise to do so.

What types of thoughts or temptations would you be wise to flee from in regard to your journey to wellness and a healthy, changed life?

____

____

____

Removing yourself physically, praying and asking God for help through His power and presence, or calling a friend are just a few of the things you can do in such a situation.

Another area Paul addresses in 2 Timothy 2 is found in verses 23-26. In your own words, how are you to deal with those who might oppose you?

____

____

____

____

If we handle opposition in this manner, they might be more willing to listen to our message.

> **_Inner Reflection: How can choosing heavenly wisdom help me experience joy and real life change?_**

DAY 6 ~ STOP AND CONSIDER

I used to ask myself why my fitness journey was so hard. Why couldn't I love working out like so many other people did? I realized that working out was a burden I had to bear, not a gift I got to enjoy. I realized that a new seed had to be planted. Maybe you have been planting the wrong seeds too. Here are a few seeds I decided to plant into my life concerning fitness.

1. The seed of variety: I tried different things until I found something I really enjoyed doing. I discovered that I enjoy most types of exercise if I have a buddy.
2. The seed of patience: For too long I set unrealistic goals for myself, which in turn caused me to fail every time and quit way too soon. Planting the seed of patience allowed me to see my fitness plan as a method of lasting life change, rather than just a method of weight loss. Don't forget you are a work in progress. Being patient allows you to start slow and develop a solid foundation of fitness, building on it according to His guidance and wisdom.
3. The seed of grace: Many times, I write Scriptures on note cards, and when I am mentally and physically exhausted, the power of Scripture allows me to push through and finish. The seed of grace allows me space to learn, grow, and even fail, but it never allows me to give up. I know His grace is sufficient for me and for you.

Don't put off till tomorrow what you need to do today. Taking care of our physical body is an act of worship unto the Lord. A fitness plan is part of the process, mentally and physically. Find some good music, a podcast, or a trainer and get focused on making some changes. Start moving until you find what you really like. Set some goals, invite a buddy along with you, and learn to have fun in the process.

Remember, in James 1:2-4 it says, "Consider it a great joy, my brothers, whenever you experience various trials, knowing that the testing of your faith produces endurance. But endurance must do its complete work so that you may be mature and complete lacking nothing."

People who take gardening seriously usually keep a gardening notebook. They keep track of details pertaining to their crop and note when to fertilize, troublesome pests and what they do about them, where they buy their plants, etc. They take care to jot down dates of when they started the seeds, transplanting times, and identifying plants. So much goes into preparing the soil and taking care of a garden.

You learned about three types of seeds that, when planted, will produce a healthy body. Name them:

Seed of ________________ Seed of ________________ Seed of ________________

Get a small notebook and title it "My Garden Seeds". At the top of the page, write the day of the week you start planting. Jot down the three seeds, leaving space between for notes. Leave room at the bottom of the page for one more seed, the seed of a critical spirit. Keep track of how you planted each one, any problems you may have had, or blessings which sprouted up during that day. If you encounter any signs of a pesky insect (a critical spirit), make an entry at the bottom of any details. Then end your day in prayer, thanking God for helping you plant the three joyful seeds, and asking for help with the insect of a critical spirit.

Your notebook can be a seasonal book or ongoing. Share with someone how it is working for you.

Inner Reflection: Am I taking care of my physical body as an act of worship unto the Lord? What seeds have I planted in my body?

CHOOSE YOUR CHALLENGE FOR THE WEEK

NUTRITION CHALLENGE—GOAL: CHANGE YOUR MIND!

1. Take a tour of your local grocery store and take some notes on shopping smarter and label reading.
2. Kick the salt. Try to not add salt while you are cooking this week. Taste your food at each meal before adding salt to any food on your plate.
3. Eat fish at least twice this week. Try having grilled fish at lunch on a sandwich or bun with a side salad.

FITNESS CHALLENGE—GOAL: CHANGE YOUR BODY!

1. As you are grocery shopping, think of adding in a few extra steps by walking around the perimeter of the store at least once before heading toward the items you need. Move in place whenever you are talking on the phone. Take a walk at lunch and after dinner. Adding just a few extra steps has a big payoff at the end of your week.
2. Calf Stretches are strength-training exercises. To do calf stretches, find a wall with nothing on it. Stand facing the wall with your hands at eye level. Place your left leg behind your right leg. Keep your left heel on the floor and bend your right knee. Hold the stretch for fifteen to thirty seconds. Repeat two to four times per leg.

LIFESTYLE CHALLENGE—GOAL: CHANGE YOUR LIFE!

1. When something stressful happens, spend a minute on deep breathing. Then ask yourself, "Is the way I'm reacting to this situation increasing my tension? Is my reaction logical and reasonable? Is there another way to view the situation?" We can begin to react differently if we give ourselves five minutes and pray. Ask the Lord if your reaction is honoring to Him. You cannot control every situation, but you can control how you react to every situation. There is a difference!

CHALLENGE I CHOSE ~ PROGRESS I MADE:

DAY 7 ~ JOURNAL PROMPT

My daily seed-sowing habits may produce…

WEEK 7
JOYFUL SURRENDER

Scripture Focus of the Week

Submit yourselves then to God. Resist the devil, and he will flee from you.

[James 4:7]

Do you believe that God has a plan for your life?

A thought I want to plant early this week is that His plan probably doesn't look like the one you have in your mind. You may be thinking, "But I like the plan I have already." Yep, me too! I like being in control. Self-sufficient people may have it all together and roll up their sleeves and work a little harder to fix the problems. However, they struggle with the seed of submission/surrender. Have you considered that we must come to a place where we recognize our plans and our lives are not our own and that they can and do change at times in a mere moment?

This week, we are going to spend time weeding out some of the problem areas that we have to submit in. Jesus will be our guide, providing the plan and the provisions for us to be successful. He has all the resources we need, and when we allow Him to take the lead, He is faithful to guide us by His Spirit and His Word.

Write out Proverbs 3:5-6.

____

____

____

____

Every time I read these verses, I have to go back and surrender my plans to the Lord. I ask Him to show me His way and to direct me down the road of grace. No matter the challenges we face, the temptations we encounter, or the past hurts we struggle to overcome, He is able to bring peace and joy to the broken places of our lives as we plant the life-changing work that submission to Him brings. God's direction is always best, and His desire is for our traveling time to be as memorable as our destination to freedom, even when we feel we are in a battle.

After reading Proverbs 2:5-6, write out a prayer of surrender to the Lord, and ask Him for direction concerning your past.

____

____

____

____

____

____

____

DAY 1 ~ INNER FIGHT

Do you ever feel like there is a war going on inside of you? I feel like that every day. In fact, there is a real fight going on in all of us. I once heard a pastor tell the story of a white dog and a black dog in a fight. Which was the winner? The one you fed the most that day. Plant this image in your mind and think of it this way: the black dog represents the flesh and our old sinful nature, and the white dog represents the spirit and our new nature. Winning our many daily battles is based on which nature we feed.

Let's read James 4:1-7.

James begins chapter four with two questions: What causes fights and quarrels among you? Don't they come from the desires that battle within you?

As James moves through the bulk of chapter four, he doesn't mince words. His honest and straightforward approach gets right to the heart of the matter: selfishness is the root of all conflict. James' main point: don't look elsewhere for the source of your conflicts, look within. Ouch!

This chapter is more reaches further than we are able to cover in this particular study, so I want to zero in on the conflict this battle seems to wage within us and how it relates to our wellness struggle and the issues with food.

Think about how many times you start a Bible reading plan, a Bible study, a new eating program, tracking your food, or an exercise workout. The intention is to start, finish, and be successful. Good intentions, but what happens if we get off track, miss a day, have too many demands placed on us, overload on family commitments, or get behind? We usually give up.

Think of the area in your own life where your inner struggle (dogfight) seems to be the greatest. ____

Who do you normally blame? ____________________

James is saying that we will never resolve this struggle/conflict until we correctly identify the source of it. We must look within and see that our own selfishness is at fault. James also emphasizes that minimizing or underestimating the power of an enemy (black dog) is a sure path toward defeat!

Write out 1 Peter 5:8.

____

____

____

____

Scripture tells us to be on guard. There is an enemy within each of us that is engaged in a fierce battle. Self versus self is at the heart of my struggle, and poses as a friend promising the easy way (pleasure, fun and enjoyment), but that way is my death, defeat, and failure.

Most of us struggle to get and stay on track with a healthy new lifestyle; all the while, we have feelings that we are not good enough, we can't meet the mark; we don't quite measure up, or we don't have what it takes. We fight an inner battle (dogfight) that is impossible to win—without God's power.

If we start the day with Him, saying, "Lord, may all I do be done today with Your power in and through my life", then we will begin to participate with the Lord. We will desire to work with Him instead of working against the Lord, allowing our own selfish desires to dominate the day. That is the seed that brings about real change.

Make time today to ask God to take control. When you settle the battle, you can count it all joy, surrendering your will and way to the Lord's control. Then watch as He begins to do amazing things in your life.

Inner Reflection: What things throw me off the plan? Can I relinquish control to God?

DAY 2 ~ A CHOICE TO BE MADE

Look up James 4:4 and fill in the blanks.

"You adulterous people, don't you know that ________________ with the world means enmity against God? Therefore, anyone who ____________ to be a ________________ of the world becomes an ____________ of God."

According to James, a choice must be made between friendship with God and friendship with the world. The significance and power of the choice is pretty clear.

Now look at Daniel 1:8. What did Daniel do?

____

____

Daniel resolved not to defile himself with the royal food and wine. Daniel made a choice, and the choice he made honored the Lord.

What about the choices you and I make? When we allow the decision we make concerning food and exercise to be brought under the Lordship of Christ, then we can begin to see change. There is power in our choice.

Are there poor choices that you have been making in your wellness journey? Consider sharing some of them here.

____

____

____

Of the poor choices you have shared, which are you choosing to change?

____

____

____

An imbalanced diet and poor food choices affects our overall health. The foods we put in our body directly impact how we feel, our weight, and our risk of developing chronic diseases. It also has a direct effect on our desire to exercise. When we are tired and sluggish, we really have no desire to exercise. Making changes to our diet and losing a moderate amount of weight can improve our blood pressure levels, lower blood cholesterol, and lessen our risk of suffering serious chronic illnesses.

The choice seems simple, but it is a battle I understand all too well. Quitting will always seem easier than finishing! Regardless of where you are in your journey, when we choose to stop and commit our wholehearted surrender to God, it changes the choices we make. Just as He equipped Daniel to stand firm, He will do the same for us. Committing our choices to God will bring joy and freedom.

Close today by reading Joshua 24:15 and Deuteronomy 30:19. Write out a prayer signifying who you will choose to follow today.

____

____

____

Inner Reflection: How often do I prepare in advance what decision I'll make?

DAY 3 ~ PROUD VERSUS HUMBLE

I had dropped out of one more health-and-wellness program again. I felt like a failure. I had a great husband, beautiful kids, and great friends. I had an active ministry at church and was running a successful produce business. From the outside, I looked like I had it all together. Except for one issue: my weight. It was impossible to hide. I had been to doctors looking for help. I tried the pills, shakes, cleanses, and diets. Nothing really worked.

The guilt and self-condemnation would become all consuming. The depression would then set in, along with the anger and hurt. No matter how hard I tried, no matter how many prayers I prayed or tears I cried, I would always default back to my food-addicted behavior patterns. Failing one more time, defeated.

I was the one who could do it all and had it all together. I had to be the one to finally confess my sin. I finally stopped trying to hide the truth. I humbly walked into a group of friends and confessed my powerlessness over food. I opened up my life to the power of God.

This is the power James points us to in James 4:6. Let's write the verse out here:

____

____

____

Humbling myself before God allowed me to finally see I only needed His approval. God's grace allowed me the freedom to plug into the power that only He could offer.

His grace is essential for our spiritual growth. It usually comes after we confess our sin and with our commitment and resolve to yield our will, mind, and body over to His will and purposes. We are then better able to hear, receive, and obey His Word.

We come to the place where we realize our need, as led by the Spirit, and then we will be better able to obey. God's grace is poured out on our lives as we humbly come asking for His help.

Is there an area of your life you have been holding back from the Lord?

____

____

Let me assure you, even if you have been too proud to ask for help, you have not outrun the grace of God. Our refusal to trust God to provide what we need and what He wants for us, along with our insistence on getting what we want for ourselves, is an act of pride. We are attempting to be the god of our own lives. God will lovingly and jealously oppose us when we do so—but He will not reject us in Christ. God is calling us back to the peaceful, faithful path of trusting Him.

Now we can take the next step and acknowledge we want Him to be in control of changing our minds and our bodies. Be all in. Let's close today by writing out a prayer asking God to help us be all in.

____

____

Inner Reflection: How will putting my energy and resources at God's disposal and trusting Him to guide me help me reach my goals?

DAY 4 ~ SUBMISSION VERSUS SURRENDER

Let's look at our Scripture focus for this week, James 4:7.

"_____________ yourselves then to God. Resist the devil and he will flee from you."

This verse begins with that tiny word *submit*. What does it mean to submit? Write out the definition:

____

____

The word *submit* is a verb, which reminds me that it is a continual action word. It means accept or yield to a superior force or to the authority or will of another person.

Now look up and write out the definition of *surrender.*

____

____

____

Surrender is used most often as a verb, and it means to relent, yield, concede, give in, or submit.

Surrender is usually used as a synonym for submission and obedience. So submit and surrender are interchangeable, which means you don't choose one or the other but use them in combination.

Surrender is where we give up or give over our rights to the authority, power, and control of Jesus, becoming usable under God's power. Submitting is when our strength and agendas are given over to God daily, which helps us stand firm because we realize God's provision for us.

Remember that initial question I asked? Do you believe God has a plan for your life? If we really want to be joyful and more content, we have to surrender control over to trusting Him and then daily submit to His direction. This allows us to take hold of the goodness, blessings, and opportunities which are ours and can only be found in Christ.

Look up Romans 8:7 and see how it relates to surrendering and submitting.

I believe the Lord wants us to realize that anything we are holding onto, anything that we are unable or unwilling to give over to Him, is likely holding onto us and probably hindering our success.

What are you holding on to?

____

____

Are you willing to do whatever is necessary to change directions?

____

____

I really wrestled with the Lord on this one, and, trust me, I worked real hard to justify all the noble reasons I could continue down this path I was on. But here is the truth: I am not going to be truly happy, content, free, and at peace until I say yes to the life-changing work that the Lord so desires to do in and through my life. I have to be *all in* by doing my part in moving toward a healthy lifestyle.

Let's do it together! Let's say, "Yes! I am all in and I am willing!"

How do we get there? Plain and simple: surrender it to the loving hands of the Father! Complete and total surrender! Romans 12:1 says, "Therefore I urge you, brethren, by the mercies of God, to present your bodies a living and Holy sacrifice, acceptable to God, which is your spiritual service of worship".

First stop is Gethsemane (a place of a submitted will to the Father) and you saying, "Lord, I am giving you full authority in my life today." (My prayer every morning.)

Second stop is Calvary (the place of a surrendered self). "Not my will but yours, Lord!"

My friend, getting here is painful, but living here is priceless. God is after our hearts but He wants our *whole* heart, not a divided one.

Let's close today by focusing on 1 Samuel 16:17. It says, "Man does not see what the Lord sees, for man sees what is visible, but the Lord sees the heart."

Inner Reflection: How often do I submit my will and surrender myself to God's plan and purpose for my life?

DAY 5 ~ RESISTING THE DEVIL

We are going to close our study time this week by digging into the last part of our Scripture focus. Let's write out James 4:7 one more time:

____

____

Now circle the words **_resist_** and **_flee_** in this verse.

There is a promise given here; however, it is clearly linked to our being willing to submit. Even though we have submitted our inner fight with our wellness journey to the Lord, there is still work to be done. We must learn to resist Satan. We must actively seek to eliminate Satan's way of thinking and behaving from our lives.

Satan, however, is so clever and powerful that no human being can successfully resist his influence apart from God's help. Therefore, the key to resisting the devil is to sincerely and consistently draw near and remain close to God.

Let's read Ephesians 6:10-13. What do we need to do to withstand the wiles of the devil?

____

Resistance requires us to actively put on the full armor of God. It demands we continually counter Satan's lies by telling ourselves the truth about God's goodness, love, and power and use the weapons He has provided for us. The devil won't remain in the presence of our submission to the truth of God's Word.

Read Ephesians 6:18. It tells us prayer is also essential to maintain our closeness to God. If the goal is to ward off Satan's effort to regain control over us, then the more our character becomes like God's perfect nature, the less Satan will feel comfortable in our presence. He will be inclined to flee from us.

The daily practice of armoring up and praying up are keys to having victory in resisting. Anger and rebellion are not of the Lord or from the Lord, but they were buried deep in my heart. Even though I was experiencing some success in weight loss, I was still angry and rebellious. I felt like I was giving up so many things and there were so many changes that needed to be made in my eating habits.

Is there a habit in your life where you know you need to resist Satan?

____

____

____

Finally, I began to resist Satan in this area of my journey by thanking the Lord for an opportunity to make healthy changes. I began to walk in a newfound freedom that was nothing short of supernatural. I simply refused to continue to be rebellious and angry about change. I decided to willingly make a positive attitude change…to submit this area of struggle to the Lord and resist the lies Satan had been telling me.

We cannot continue to do negative things and expect to get positive results. Through the devastating circumstances of being overweight for the greatest part of my life, I have seen deliverance by my Deliverer, healing by my Healer, provision by my Provider, and comfort from my Comforter.

The things God taught me in these dark places, I would never have known or learned any other place. He has proven Himself and shown His character in these tough places. When we submit our lives to God's control, resist Satan, and draw close to the Lord, we grow through the pain. When we depend on Him, He becomes our Life!

Inner Reflection: Am I aware of the work God is doing in my life right now? How do I respond?

DAY 6 ~ STOP AND CONSIDER

Are you struggling with failure? The truth is, there is nothing wrong with failing. We all struggle and fail at times, but *failure* is another story. Failure only happens if we don't get back up. Look at it this way: On the road to Golgotha, when Jesus stumbled and fell, His strength was failing Him. What if He had not gotten back up? Where would you and I be today? When He looked to the cross that day, it was for the hope of what you and I would become because of His struggle.

His victory at the cross is what can empower us to get up and continue to move forward now. Sometimes we hesitate to continue the journey because we are seeing no results. But, if we maintain a heavenly perspective, we will realize we may not see the good from our effort until later. We must claim a victory we cannot see, based on faith in our Lord. Paul tells us in 1 Corinthians 15:58 to be steadfast, immovable always abounding in the work of the Lord.

Life change has to become important to you in order to succeed! When you have been making the wrong choices so long, it seems the normal thing to do. What is truly right seems abnormal to a mind set on defeat and rebellion. God uses the hard, dark places in our lives to refine us, grow us, and make us more like Him.

Take time today to evaluate where you are in your journey. Write out some new goals in the space below. Spend time this week praying about them, and then write out a plan you can use to resist Satan's attack as you move forward.

Where I am at:

____

____

____

New goals:

____

____

____

Action plan to resist Satan's attack:

____

____

____

____

Inner Reflection: What does surrender look like in my life right now?

CHOOSE YOUR CHALLENGE FOR THE WEEK

NUTRITION CHALLENGE—GOAL: CHANGE YOUR MIND!

1. When eating breakfast, focus on whole grains with at least 5 grams of fiber per serving. A nice, warm, whole grain wrap with egg and cheese or ham will do it. Remember, think lean and healthy!

2. If the drive-thru is your breakfast plan and it's on your way to work, look for the most healthy and protein-packed choice you can find. Breakfast is a great place to fuel up your day, so make the calories you are choosing count. Stay away from high-fat and sugary foods for breakfast. These are empty calories!

3. Add some fresh fruit to your oatmeal or cereal. A tablespoon of flaxseed meal will add some healthy fat. Make your breakfast choice more balanced and nutrient-packed.

FITNESS CHALLENGE—GOAL: CHANGE YOUR BODY!

1. A stability ball is a great way to get an intense back workout. Stand up tall, using good posture, and place a stability ball so it's positioned in between your midback and a wall behind you. Your feet should be held shoulder-width apart and about 12 to 18 inches away from the wall in order to maintain proper balance. While keeping your spine in this position, lean into the ball by pivoting only at your ankle joints. Hold for a count of five seconds before relaxing. After a few seconds, repeat the hold until you feel your back and/or leg muscles fatigue. Try to work up to 15 to 20 repetitions of the exercise each day.

2. Vary your exercise and try to have fun. Take a walk one day, lift weights the next, ride a bike, swim, or play basketball or handball. Watching TV while moving your body can help take the tediousness out of exercise and give you something to look forward to during that time. Find some bands and small hand weights to use during TV time.

LIFESTYLE CHALLENGE GOAL: CHANGE YOUR LIFE!

1. Our nighttime routines influence our ability to fall asleep and experience a night of quality sleep and restorative rest. Sleep is designed to restore, recalibrate, and renew our brain and body functions. Some simple tips to help you get started with a better night's rest: make sure your room temperature is a little cooler than daytime temperature, wake up and go to bed at the same time each day, and avoid all

technology for at least an hour before bedtime. This hour each night would be a great time to incorporate some realization therapy, reading, or mediating. This would also be a great time to create and use a thankfulness journal, jotting down all the things you are thankful for that day.

CHALLENGE I CHOSE ~ PROGRESS I MADE:

____

____

____

____

____

____

____

____

____

____

____

____

____

____

DAY 7 ~ JOURNAL PROMPT

In my mind, is surrender positive or negative?

WEEK 8
PASSION FOR OTHERS

Scripture Focus of the Week

If anyone, then, knows the good they ought to do and doesn't do it, it is sin for them.

[James 4:17]

I will forever remember the group of ladies that were in my accountability group in the early days of my weight-loss journey. Even though I was the largest woman in the group, I never felt embarrassed or excluded. They welcomed me with open arms. I was the most emotional group member; I always cried at weigh-ins. Loss or gain, I cried. Many times they cried with me, but they always encouraged me. I was the biggest loser, but all I ever saw on their faces was joy for my success. My success became their success. They were so proud of me and all that I accomplished. They grieved with me, prayed over me, and celebrated with me at every milestone. They all had a passion to see me be successful in this journey. They exhibited a passion for my success that changed my life.

Some years later, I began to model the same passion for others that had been modeled for me. In the first wellness group I led, the Lord sent me Amanda. She was very quiet, faithful to class, had a very unbalanced lifestyle, and for medical reasons needed to lose weight. Our group decided to sign up for a 5K together and Amanda joined in. This was the first race she had ever attempted and she was slow. She was so slow that the police and fire truck were right behind her in the race. There were four of us in the lead, and when we finished, instead of celebrating in our victory we went back for Amanda. She started crying when she saw us. We walked with her all the way through the finish line. I told her she must be a pretty special person to have a police escort all the way to the finish. She finished last that day, but she finished! That race changed her life.

Amanda told me later that at no point in her life had anyone ever come back for her and when she looked up and saw us coming she realized she could trust us. From that point on, Amanda let the walls down that had been the barriers to her freedom and success. She is now the encourager to many in our group. She is finding a healthy, balanced life as she changes her mind and learns what it really means to change her body with healthy food and exercise.

This week, as we move through the next verses in James, we will look at some things we need to avoid in our journey to wellness and explore ways we can develop a genuine passion for others that produces love, joy, and peace in us…and, yes, life change in others. Real and lasting!

DAY 1 ~ ABOVE THE LAW

Let's begin by reading our text for the week, James 4:8-17.

Write out verse 11 below:

____

____

____

James appeals to us as family, asking that we not slander one another.

What does the word *slander* mean to you?

____

____

When I look up the definition this is what I find: 1. the utterance of false charges or misrepresentations which defame and damage another's reputation 2: A false and defamatory oral statement about or to a person

Do a little self-evaluation concerning your wellness journey. Examine your attitudes and actions toward others. Be honest with yourself.

Are you jealous when others lose weight and you don't?

____

Are there times that you are critical of others' attempts to lose weight?

____

Do you feel superior when you lose weight and others don't?

____

Are you an encourager regardless of the number on the scales?

____

Do you build others up or tear them down?

____

Now read Romans 13:10. What two things does this verse say love does?

____

____

When we fail to love, we are actually breaking God's law and setting ourselves above the law of love. Learning to be an encourager like the ladies in my group were is a learned behavior and must be practiced on a regular basis to become a natural part of our lifestyle.

Saying and doing something beneficial to others will cure you of finding fault and increase your ability to obey the law of love. Learning to love Amanda the way God loves Amanda changed her, but it also changed me. Amanda crossed the finish line with tears of joy streaming down her face not because she had won, but because she finished. In the process, she found friends she could trust with her deepest hurts and failures…friends she could be real with, who loved her in her imperfections. What a beautiful picture of living out the law of love, not putting ourselves above it.

Take some time today to reflect on someone in your sphere of influence that needs your encouragement and friendship. It could be someone who has been difficult to get to know. Pray and ask the Lord to guide you to be an encourager to someone in your church, accountability group, or your Bible study class this week.

Inner Reflection: God's love changes me from the inside out.

DAY 2 ~ PRESUMPTEOUS PLANS

Let's begin today by reading James 4:13-17.

In verse 14, James makes a bold statement to us: "Why, you do not even know what will happen tomorrow. What is your _________________?"

What is your life? Let's camp out here a bit. Life is short and fragile, no matter how many years we live. James gives a warning here, telling us not to be deceived into thinking that we have lots of remaining time to live. Even though my friend, Susan, lived ready, I am sure she never anticipated that her life would end at such an early age. Death was not on her radar.

What things have you focused on lately, thinking you'll have plenty of time later?

____

____

____

A few examples that come to my mind are: When my schedule slows down, I will make time for meal planning and eating healthy. When I lose this weight, I will be happy and get back to living. When I get through school, I will take more time for my kids or grandkids. When I get the next promotion and things settle down at work; I will have more time to work on my exercise program.

I wonder how many God-appointments we have missed in this journey of life by our busyness. Let's just call it as it is. Busyness is sin, and it is also the tool that Satan uses to distract us from the purpose God has designed us for. I need to be reminded on a regular basis that life is a journey toward a destination, but life is not the destination. A life lived for Christ is truly a life well-lived.

As part of this life-changing journey, we know it is very important to make plans, but we always want to keep Christ at the center of all we do and the plans we make. I remember my leader continually telling me to pray about it: Pray about every obstacle, every challenge, every idea, and every thought. She continually pointed me to the center point of life: JESUS.

Look up Jeremiah 29:11. What does this verse tell us that God knows and has for us?

____

God has and knows the plans He has for us and He even says they are plans to prosper us and not to harm us, plans to give us hope and a future.

Let's begin to put God's plans and desires at the center of our planning and pray about each change we need to make in our wellness journey.

> **Inner Reflection: Have I asked God about my exercise and eating plans and allowed Him to be the center point of all I do today and every day?**

DAY 3 ~ ARROGANT BOASTING

Let's begin today by re-reading our Scripture from yesterday (James 4:13-17).

Write out verse 16:

____

____

____

Now go back and circle the words **you** and **boasting** and then underline the words **arrogant** and **evil**.

How do you feel when you hear someone boasting about their accomplishments?

____

____

All of us tend to boast from time to time. It makes us feel better about ourselves. Today we need to become aware that boasting is rooted in pride and is another tool that Satan uses to causes us to lose sight of the good plans the Lord has for us. Exalting ourselves in such a way that we are flaunting our gifts, abilities, knowledge, or accomplishments are all forms of boasting.

What about in our wellness journey? When we are being successful at losing weight, eating right, and exercising, it is so easy to take the credit for our success. But when we confess our dependency on Christ, it allows Him to receive the credit for our success.

What does God want from us? How about the following ABC plan:

A. Make plans with the intent of obeying the will of God first in all we do. Our plan is good, but God's plan is better.

Write out Proverbs 19:21:

____

____

B. Speak of any human plans with the awareness that God may well intervene in them if they are not His will, and if He does, that is okay.

Write out Micah 6:8:

____

____

C. Develop an attitude of trust in Him and live every moment in dependence on Him. Let's face it! Any other attitude is sinful, arrogant, and shortsighted.

Write out Proverbs 3:5:

____

____

Let's spend some time evaluating ourselves in an effort to recognize ways in which we may be prideful or boastful. Take time to write about any areas of your plan that need to be re-committed to the Lord and any areas of sin He might reveal to you.

____

____

____

____

Close today by writing out 1 Corinthians 13:4-7.

____

____

____

____

Inner Reflection: Boasting is rooted in pride and is another tool that Satan uses to causes me to lose sight of the good plans the Lord has for me.

DAY 4 ~ KNOWING AND DOING

There is a saying that people who fail to plan, plan to fail. It is foundational to success to have a plan. There are many tools out there that help us in our wellness journey.

Here are some tools that have helped me be very successful in my journey: food journals, exercise logs, prayer journals, emotional mapping workbooks, menu planning guides, grocery lists, healthy recipes, Garmin watches, I-Pod with music, portion control plates, accountability groups and workout buddies.

These tools were all designed to help me be successful. The key is *I have to use them.* If we know what we should do, then why don't we do it? We seem to easily get distracted and off track.

Paul gives us some insight in Romans 7:15. What does he say?

____

____

Paul exposes in the passage the very weakness of our flesh as the root problem which prevents us from living the kind of lives God requires and which we desire in our innermost being. Paul is honest and real, exposing the weakness of our flesh, which we all share. Paul points us to our only hope, found in God's provision for godly living.

Now take a moment and write out James 4:17:

____

____

We know doing wrong is sin, but James tells us sin is also not doing right when we know what is right. Now James is really meddling in our business.

The clear message here is that we are continually doing wrong even when we don't mean to and we are incapable of living out a life of doing right without the indwelling power of the Holy Spirit within us. The flesh is weak and sin is evil. We do not have the strength, but because of Christ within us we can do all things.

Write out the following Scriptures:

Philippians 3:14

____

____

John 8:32

____

____

The Lord and His purpose are perfect, but we are not. We are inundated daily with choices and decisions, doubts and fears, and many times they keep us from living out the purpose that He has established for us. We can overcome this and find the joy James talks about.

We do this by developing a plan for success, which should include consistently reading and studying His Word, prayer, and establishing healthy relationships that are designed to strengthen our faith.

Inner Reflection: I am made stronger day by day as I rise up and allow the Lord's power and strength to defeat the enemy that resides in me.

DAY 5 ~ GOD'S DIRECTION IS ALWAYS BEST

James' consistent theme through the fourth chapter has been the idea that genuine faith is proved by action. However high and lofty our view of God's law might be, a failure to do it says to the world that we do not in fact put much store by it. James is very clear that God's direction is always best. He has the entire plan already worked out, and when we trust Him, He will lead us by His Word and Spirit. No matter the challenges we face, the temptations we endure or the hurts we must overcome in this fractured life, He will bring us peace and joy.

Let's look at what James tells us in verse 17 one more time. To know the right thing to do and not do it is ___________.

When I began my weight-loss journey, I had very little hope that any program was going to work. I had tried so hard to lose weight so many times without much success. It was a step of faith in the beginning, trusting the Lord to provide because I was told to pray about everything. The paths I had always taken in the past had left me overwhelmed, frustrated, and defeated. This time, the route was different and so was the outcome.

Earlier this week, we looked up Proverbs 3:5-6. Write it one more time.

____

____

God's direction and plan changed my life and is still changing my life. Is God nudging you toward an alternate route or plan? Let's look at a few common areas of sin that might just be roadblocks or detours to your success.

Selfish Pride: leads to broken relationships.

Action: Is God leading you do your part to restore a broken relationship? Is there someone you have avoided but God is now directing you to render a service or kind word to them?

____

____

____

Pet Sins: Think about anything that hinders your time with the Lord. What is distracting you from spending time in the Word or in worship? The Bible says sin is anything that comes before the Lord.

Action: Ask for forgiveness, confess your lack of commitment to following God's plan, and then allow Him to renew and refresh your time with Him.

____

____

____

Shortcuts: Have you been taking shortcuts in your wellness journey? Cutting short your Bible time on a daily basis, hitting the drive-thru instead of cooking, not making time for an exercise routine that is beneficial to your success, or cutting your prayer time with the Lord?

Action: Turn around. God has a path of repentance ready and waiting for you. Start over and let Jesus be the center point on the new route.

____

____

____

As we close this week, take some time to pray and reflect back over any area or sin which might be hindering your success in your wellness journey. I want to challenge you to look at this journey as a *life change*. Is your passion for Jesus changing? Weight loss is a by-product of the other things that are happening and developing in our lives.

Inner Reflection: When I allow God to be the lead, I will find that He is able to use all the things in my life, even the detours and valleys, for joy.

DAY 6 ~ STOP AND CONSIDER

Finding and keeping a healthy balance has been a long and difficult process. I stand amazed at how far I have come over the last few years, but I also know that my success would not have been possible without the help and guidance of others who had a passion to see me succeed.

Life in itself is not an easy journey, but when we pair up the power we find in Christ with the love of and for others, this can become a joyful journey. Not easy, but possible. I think often of my sweet friend, Susan, who is now running the streets of Heaven. I keep a photo on my desk of the two of us, and at times when I miss her most, I look at that photo and am so reminded of her passion for Jesus and others. It gives me the strength to keep going.

Jesus exhibited a passion for others as well. He drew them in, taught them, fed them, prayed for them, and, even when they were a great disappointment; He showed them love, forgiveness, and compassion. He has done the same for each of us.

That love and passion Jesus exhibited for others led Him through much suffering and then all the way to the cross. Jesus came to earth for the purpose of laying down His life for us. He never wavered from it. Jesus' passion was due to a settled purpose.

Write a prayer here, and let's begin each morning with this prayer, asking God to reveal to us His purposes for the day.

____

____

____

Take time this next week to journal the plans He reveals to you. Make note of other things He guides you to change in your daily time with Him.

____

____

____

Inner Reflection: There is great joy in finding my purpose that is rooted in Jesus. Keeping the law of love shows others that my faith is vital and real.

CHOOSE YOUR CHALLENGE FOR THE WEEK

NUTRITION CHALLENGE—GOAL: CHANGE YOUR MIND!

1. Say no to supersizing. Anytime you eat out, resist the idea or temptation of supersizing.
2. Don't eat while engaged in other activities (watching TV, reading, and so forth). Eat only at the table, not at the fridge or while standing. You will most likely discover you naturally eat less and enjoy your food more when you eat mindfully.
3. Eat on smaller plates. Whether at home or work, make an effort to eat on a salad plate instead of a dinner plate. You will be surprised at how much less food you will eat overall.

FITNESS CHALLENGE—GOAL: CHANGE YOUR BODY!

1. Pick up the pace while doing household chores. Turn on your favorite music to help keep you moving.
2. Reward your workout time this week with a treat. Do not use food as the reward, though. Rewards are very important when it comes to an exercise program, and in some cases they can be crucial. Provide rewards that will keep you motivated and on track. New shoes or clothes, a massage, or a special trip to an event that you want to go to are all great suggestions that work.

LIFESTYLE CHALLENGE—GOAL: CHANGE YOUR LIFE!

1. This week, we are going to turn our focus to others. Ask God to give you the name of someone who needs you to encourage them. Think of others who have taken the time to encourage you and send them a thank-you note expressing your gratitude for their love and concern just when you needed it the most. Develop an attitude of gratitude for others.

CHALLENGE I CHOSE ~ PROGRESS I MADE:

DAY 7 ~JOURNAL PROMPT

Maintaining a healthy balance in my life is important because…

WEEK 9
PATIENCE IN THE PROCESS

Scripture Focus of the Week

You too, be patient and stand firm, because the Lord's coming is near.

[James 5:8]

Patience is almost a thing of the past, and after standing in the check-out line at the grocery, mine is pretty low.

Life contains a great deal of impatience and stress. Our days have others needing us or wanting something from us: spouses, children, grandchildren, aging parents, co-workers, bosses, fellow church members, and even friends and extended family. Most of the time, this fast-lane lifestyle can leave us feeling defeated and tired. Because we are constantly inundated with unhealthy food choices, giving up on a healthy lifestyle is easy. Sometimes we think it's easier to be unhealthy than to spend the time, effort, and money to be healthy.

Do you ever get impatient with yourself in this journey? We all do. If not, we wouldn't have to start over so much. Most of us are tired of starting over too. Moving forward, regardless of our pace, allows us to learn patience with ourselves and to understand how God weaves life events, including our past and present pain, into a glorious tapestry for His glory and our good. Pursuing balance is an ongoing process for all of us if we want to finish and finish well.

This week, as we walk through some of the verses in James chapter five, we will take some time to evaluate some of our attitudes and actions. Then we'll focus on areas we need to be patient with ourselves or maybe with others in this process. By God's strength, we will not only learn to patiently walk, but run in freedom!

DAY 1 ~ LIVING INDULGENTLY

Let's begin this week by reading James 5:1-4.

After reading this passage, my first thought was "Oh, James is not talking to me. I'm not rich, so I'm off the hook." Wrong. We are all rich by the standard set here, but let's take the time to look a little deeper.

Think of a time when someone blessed you by some unexpected financial generosity. This may be something you want to share at your next group meeting.

____

____

____

____

When I was a single mother, my pastor's wife unexpectedly started giving me one-hundred dollars after Christmas so I could take my little daughter to the store for a special day of shopping. I was surprised and thankful, and the money given with a pure heart allowed me to bless my little girl for several years when we had very little.

All these years later, my daughter and I continue giving the gift of one-hundred dollars to other single moms at Christmas each year. My pastor's wife modeled a Christ-centered life even though she gave me money. Her gift changed me, and it continues to change the lives of other single moms all these years later.

James' words are merely a warning to us as believers: sizable wealth or not, we tend to base our security on wealth rather than on God. Anxiety and stress over money may cause us to lead a wealth-centered life, driving us away from our true security in Christ. There is nothing wrong with owning earthly possessions. We just have to be mindful they do not own us.

Look up Hebrews 13:5 and Matthew 6:24. What do they tell us about the love of money?

____

____

____

How can money keep you from doing things God wants you to do?

____

____

In what ways may you need to change your attitude about money?

____

____

We have spent countless dollars on potions, pills, and gadgets of all descriptions to help us lose weight (or so we hoped), and yet, we often feel dissatisfied and joyless, or experience very little weight loss. The weight-loss industry is a 70.3 billion-dollar industry, and yet 70 percent of adults in our society are still overweight.

All the while, the Lord is calling us to a Christ-centered life of balance. Money and food are not our real problem. It is the attitude of the heart. When we trust Him to provide all we need, He lavishly provides.

Take time to read 1 John 3:1. You may want to record your thoughts here as you read and meditate.

____

____

____

Inner Reflection: I want eyes to see the eternal treasure that God wants to pour so abundantly into my life.

DAY 2 ~ HOARDING HURTS

Today, let's read James 5:1-9.

When you think of being self-indulgent, what comes to your mind?

____

____

____

This is the definition I found: Indulging one's own desires, passions, whims, etc., especially without restraint or excessive or unrestrained gratification of one's own appetites, desires, or whims.

Today, I want us to look at being self-indulgent from another perspective. If asked if anyone has been hurt by someone, feelings or otherwise, I am sure we can all say a resounding yes. Hurts are a part of life. When we hoard our hurts, though, it becomes an unhealthy environment where Satan often isolates us, making us weak and ineffective at living out our purpose with joy.

Let's look at the definition of a hoarder: Hoarding is an excessive accumulation of items, regardless of actual value.

My mom is a hoarder and, bless her soul, she keeps everything. Because of her excessive accumulation of stuff, when I go to her house I want to clean the place up, which stresses her out, and then I get stressed. After spending time at her home, I want to go clean my own house, which is already clean and orderly. This desire is birthed out of fear that I might become a hoarder.

So why is it so easy for me to be an emotional hoarder? Emotional hoarding is the inability to let go of intangible things which clutter up our heart, soul, and mind. It is the emotional junk we hang on to that can't be easily seen, which infects our emotions, thoughts, and behavior. It is also a place of overindulgence and, as James points out, a place of sin.

Let's look at the list of the effects of hoarding our hurts. In the second column, write out a plan that you think could help you overcome this particular hurt. Change can happen with a game plan. Take some time in class this week to share game plans and gather new options for success in the area of hoarding hurts.

Effects of Hoarding	Game Plan for Resolution
Isolation	________________________________
Strained Relationships	________________________________
Unsafe Environment	________________________________
Regret and Discouragement	________________________________
Guilt and Anger	________________________________

List any new ideas you gained in class or your quiet time:

____

____

____

I would not even consider being a physical hoarder, but as an emotional hoarder I stockpiled many traumatic memories, hurtful words, and heartbreaks, past and present. When I would try to declutter and break free, Satan would use them to keep me isolated.

Many of my issues with my weight have been directly related to emotional hoarding. When I would try to lose weight to please others or to gain their love and acceptance, I would end up lonely and defeated, always giving up and giving in. I used food to medicate the pain. I allowed food to be my comfort and friend; all the while I was looking for love and acceptance. I felt I needed to live up to an invisible standard of perfection that was never said verbally but was implied by actions and attitudes. Through the process of using emotional mapping, I have found freedom and understanding that food was never meant to be my comfort or friend. It was made to nourish my body for His service. I have been bought with a price, and I am precious to Him. Spending time daily in prayer, Bible study, and worship is the key to safeguarding my heart from hoarding hurts.

As we close today, stop and consider the warning in the verses below. Spend time in prayer about any hurts you may be hoarding. Write your thoughts here or in your journal or share them with a friend.

____

____

____

"There is a grievous evil which I have seen under the sun: riches being hoarded by their owner to his hurt." Ecclesiastes 5:13

"Your gold and silver are corroded. Their corrosion will testify against you and eat your flesh like fire. You have hoarded wealth in the last days." James 5:3

Inner Reflection: God is faithful to free me from the past and guide my steps in the present.

DAY 3 ~ A FARMER'S SECRET

Let's begin today by writing out James 5:7.

____

____

____

I used to live on a farm, but I was a happy girl when we moved to the city. Farming is hard work. As an adult, I have a new respect for farmers and the hard work they perform day in and day out. There are many life lessons about work and patience to be learned from farmers.

Our Scripture reading today mentions how the farmer patiently waits for the land to yield its valuable crop. He cannot hurry the process. He doesn't take time off, hoping for a good crop to harvest. He is steadily working at it. The farmer lives by faith, looking toward the future reward of an abundant crop.

The same principle can be applied to our wellness journey. Most of us started with a goal in mind of losing some weight, making time for exercise, or a host of other healthy changes. Have you been steadily working at it?

Yes _______________   No_______________   Sometimes _______________

Have you taken time off, hoping for good results with only halfhearted effort?

Yes _______________   No_______________

If you answered yes to the second question, what results did you get?

____

Developing patience with ourselves and with others allows us to stay on track with our health and wellness goals. We put what we learn into practice and do it over and over again until it's a habit. We are living by faith, praying, and trusting the Lord for the abundant harvest of life change in us, but in the same way as the farmer, we must do the hard work that consistently follows our plan. Doing is believing!

How does knowing that Jesus will return give you hope?

____

____

Both the farmer and the Christian must live by faith, looking toward the future rewards of their labors. Let us, like the farmer, work faithfully to build lasting treasure in the kingdom of God. He is coming in due season, just like the farmer's crop.

As we close today, think of some ways you can practice building treasure in the kingdom of God.

____

____

____

Inner Reflection: God enables me to live out the life He has called me to live and I have dreamed of living. He helps me to be strong and of good courage.

DAY 4 ~STAND FIRM

Begin by writing James 5:8.

____

____

Circle the two directives that James gives us in this verse.

The first directive James give us is to be patient. Consider patience as an exercise of self-control that shows you can handle life when times get tough.

What are some negative things that happen when we are impatient?

____

____

____

Impatience causes me to make poor decisions, wastes my time and energy, and puts me under a great deal of stress.

Patience, on the other hand, helps me to be persistent and stay in the race for the long haul. It prompts me to think of others and their happiness, gives me self-control, and allows me freedom from stress. Because of patience, I can be more flexible and easily acknowledge there are some things that are just out of my control.

I did start praying about my patience attitude. I asked the Lord how I could change my attitude at the grocery standing in the check-out line. I know it is a small thing, but my attitude was not reflecting the Jesus who lives in me. He directed me to view going to the grocery as a character-building time and an opportunity to pray for others. As of late, I have been caught smiling more, have been less stressed-out, and will pray for someone in the checkout line. That is a good thing!

The second directive that James gives us is to stand firm.

What is the Lord calling you to stand firm in?

____

____

When I feel overwhelmed by life's temptations, I now turn to the Lord. His strength protects me so that I am able to stand firm and continue on the path He has set before me.

Some days our desire to quit, give up, give in, and go back will seem overwhelming, but that is when we must stand firm. Taking the next right step forward is an act of patient obedience. Praying and asking for God's help is standing firm. Choosing to put one foot in front of the other is an act of sacrificial love, and when we cannot run, we resolve to walk by faith. At this point, it stops being about us and starts being about Him and what He wants to do through us.

Close today by writing out Philippians 1:27.

____

____

____

____

Inner Reflection: If I were as patient with myself as God is toward me, how would my life be different?

DAY 5 ~ NO GRUMBLING ALLOWED

Let's read James 5:9-12.

When things go wrong, we may complain and blame others for our miseries and failures. Blaming others is easier than owning our share of the responsibility, but it can be both destructive and sinful.

Job's life is a beautiful picture of patient perseverance and the compassion and mercy of the Lord. It also teaches a hard lesson about grumbling.

A brief overview of the book of Job shows us that God considered Job a man perfect and upright in all his ways. God allowed Satan to test Job by attacking him in multiple ways. Job cried out to God, and against all odds believed God. Job exhibited trust in the goodness of God and waited patiently on God. Suffering is part of life, but if, like Job, we continue to seek the Lord and trust Him, He will show us at some point how He is using that for His glory and our good.

Is there an area in your wellness journey that you have been grumbling about?

____

____

For me, it was the process of recording my food daily. I just thought it was a waste of valuable time. I didn't eat much…or I ate the same thing day in and day out. Have you ever used those excuses? After a season of the Lord working on me, I began to track my food. I gave a copy to my accountability partner weekly. I have now been recording my food for many years (yes, I still do). As a personal trainer with a certification in fitness nutrition, I have come to realize the true importance of tracking my food daily.

What was the difference? Obedience. I realized God's love language was obedience. I wanted to openly show my gratitude to God for all He was doing in and through my life.

God uses the hard, dark places in our lives to refine us, grow us, and to make us more like Him, just like He did with Job.

Through the devastating circumstances of being overweight for the greatest part of my life, I have seen God's faithful provision. The things God has taught me in these dark places I would never have known or learned any other place. He has proved His character in these tough places. We get to choose to grumble about our circumstances or stick around and remain faithful and be patient. When we depend on Him, He becomes life!

What areas of your journey or plan do you need to bring in honest surrender to the Lord so He can begin to restore you?

____

____

____

Inner Reflection: It is always easier to blame others than to acknowledge where I am.

DAY 6 ~ STOP AND CONSIDER

It is so easy for us to become impatient because we live in a very fast-paced world. We want fast service, fast food, the fastest internet. We want immediate resolutions to our weight-loss issues. We want exercise to be easy and meals that are super-fast, delicious, and healthy! We are to the point that we can buy almost everything online, including groceries, because we don't have time to go to the store. We want what we want, and we want it now!

Then I look inward at all the places where I am impatient with myself. I have this idea that I should be perfect, but life is not perfect and sometimes it isn't pretty. It is hard and difficult. It is messy and painful, and following a regimented eating and exercise plan is sometimes very difficult. Honestly, I struggle. We all struggle but we *cannot* quit.

In the early years of my struggle with my weight, I believed God could just zap me and keep me from eating and make me lose weight. In my mind it was really just that simple. Yet I struggled so many years before freedom came, and even now I can say it has been a painful journey. It was one of the hardest things I have ever gone through. I can also say that God has been faithful. I now realize my exit plan from obesity was designed so that He would receive all the glory. God wants to be glorified through us. That brings joy.

Are you allowing God to be glorified through your life?

Yes ___________ No____________ Sometimes ________

Do you believe God is able to __________________? (Fill in the blank)

____________Yes ____________No __________Not Sure

Example: I believe God is able to save my lost family members. I believe God is able to guide me to make healthy choices.

Our responsibility is our faith response to Jesus' ability. We have the opportunity to walk in daily victory by trusting Jesus with the outcome, as well as patiently moving forward and making daily progress.

Write out a prayer to the Lord asking Him to guide you to confessing areas in your life where you have not trusted Him fully. Write out your 'I believe God prayers' on post cards and pray over them regularly.

____

____

____

____

CHOOSE YOUR CHALLENGE FOR THE WEEK

NUTRITION CHALLENGE—GOAL: CHANGE YOUR MIND!

1. Make or order omelets, sandwiches, wraps, and burritos with veggies added. Lighten up on sauces and condiments and add the beauty of the rainbow to those meals.
2. Use leaf or romaine lettuce for sandwiches or wraps rather than carb-rich bread. Just add your meat and veggies straight to the lettuce. It is amazing how good lettuce wraps can be.
3. Top your baked potatoes with steamed vegetables instead of gravy, meat, or cheese.

FITNESS CHALLENGE—GOAL: CHANGE YOUR BODY!

1. TV can be fattening—so turn it off! Are you a couch potato or computer addict? Limit your TV and computer hours and plan healthy physical activities. Get outside and get moving!
2. By now you should be spending at least 30 to 60 minutes a day in some type of exercise activity, which should include some strength training. If not, it's never too late to start.
3. It is important to dress for success. Comfort above all else counts when it comes to shoes and clothes for exercising. As you start your exercise routine, make sure that your body is well supported. This means comfortable shoes that are a good quality and clothes that are comfortable and fit well.

LIFESTYLE CHALLENGE—GOAL: CHANGE YOUR LIFE!

1. Learn to be aware of eating habits and behaviors that lead to overeating. Also focus on social and emotional situations that lead you to snack compulsively. A food tracker or journal helps you see exactly what you eat and drink throughout the day. Also consider arranging some moral support! Beware of family or friends that are saboteurs who discourage you from adopting a healthier lifestyle.

CHALLENGE I CHOSE ~ PROGRESS I MADE:

DAY 7 ~ JOURNAL PROMPT

Developing an attitude of gratitude for me is…

WEEK 10
JOY IN THE JOURNEY

Scripture Focus of the Week

Therefore, confess your sins to each other and pray for each other so that you may be healed. The prayer of a righteous person is powerful and effective.

[James 5:16]

I was at the beach in late November, walking by the shoreline. There was no storm on the horizon, but the wind was so strong it was blowing the sand. It was like little darts hitting my feet and legs. After a very short distance, it became so painful that I gave up and went inside. No joy in that walk.

Consider how small a grain of sand is. Now think about the little things in our lives that rob us of joy every day. You worked late, you're tired, you had a fight with your spouse, you're sick, your kids or grandkids have a ball game, you develop an injury, you don't like the temperature they keep the church, you're not happy with the pastor, you went on vacation, you had to work out of town a few weeks or on a weekend, a dear friend is in the hospital, there was a birthday party for someone at work, there was a death in the family, it's raining, it's just too cold…the list can go on and on.

Little grains of stress, discontent, dissatisfaction, a poor choice here and a bad choice there—and one morning you wake up late and decide quiet time is too much effort, eating right and making healthy choices is just not as easy as it used to be. Exercise has become like work again. You allowed little grains of sand (the little foxes, as the Bible calls them) to begin to deteriorate what has been accomplished in your life. Those little sins, disturbances, or interruptions that rob us of the joy in this journey are the very things that cause the greatest problems and must not be ignored but identified and addressed if we are to continue to be successful at real life change!

Living a transformed life with joy is worth the effort. As we wrap up our study in James, let's consider how we might experience real joy in the journey, as well as at the finish, as James guides us to a powerful life of confession and prayer.

DAY 1~ PRAYING WITH FAITH

Let's begin our study time today by reading James 5:13-20.

As believers, our most powerful resource is a relationship with God that is built on prayer. Many times we see prayer as a last resort to be tried when all else fails, but this approach is backwards. Prayer should come first, and if we begin and end each day with prayer, our lives will not only be more joy-filled, but more powerful and effective.

Look up and write out what the following Scriptures say about prayer.

Philippians 4:6: "Do not be anxious about anything, but in every situation, by _____________ and _______________, with thanksgiving, present your requests to God."

Colossians 4:2: "Devote yourselves to _____________, being _____________ and _____________"

1 Thessalonians 5:17: "_____________ continually"

Romans 12:12: "Be _____________ in hope, _____________ in affliction, faithful in _____________"

Romans 8:2: "In the same way, the Spirit helps us in our _______________. We do not know what we ought to _________ for, but the Spirit himself intercedes for us through wordless groans."

Stop! Drop! Pray! When you need help, follow that plan. It includes what you eat and drink and if you exercise. Then you will learn to talk with God on an intimate level about everything.

Do you have a problem or need? Are you praying, or just talking about it? Take time to have someone pray with you concerning it. Thank God for hearing your prayers, and then, in faith, trust Him to bring about His solution in His time. His desire is not for us to fret or worry but to pray.

Close your time today by writing out a prayer of thanksgiving to the Lord.

____

____

Inner Reflection: Praying and trusting God will break down barriers.

DAY 2 ~ PRAYING THROUGH TRIALS

This wellness journey and life in general is made up of mistakes, learning, waiting, growing, practicing patience, and being persistent. In the very beginning of the book of James, he tells us to consider it all joy as we encounter trials of various kinds. James didn't say we might, but **when**. He is letting us know up front that life is like traveling a treacherous road. There are potholes that jolt us, detours that get us off course, and signs warning us of danger ahead that at times we listen to and at times we ignore.

Through it all, God offers us daily strength and guidance through prayer. Praying through trials brings us to a closer and deeper relationship with our Lord.

How can prayer take us through trials?

____

____

How exactly do we pray as we seek to find wellness and instead find difficulty?

____

____

Let's read Psalm 39:12.

What is the psalmist asking for?

____

____

When we cry out to God for help as we go through difficulties, He hears us and because He loves us, will respond. It may not be as we want or expect, but we can be sure it's according to His plan. Whose plan is better, yours or God's?

____

Of course, God's is better. That fact should bring joy into your heart and help you go through the difficulty. Keeping a prayer log is helpful during such times. When God provides the answer to your problem, record it next to the prayer. When the next difficulty comes (and it will), you can look back and know God was there and God will continue to be there.

When we pray, we experience more joy in our lives. Write out how you can increase prayer in your life as you journey toward a healthy lifestyle.

____

____

____

One thing I continue to do that helps increase my prayer life is to set my watch to alarm every day at 2:10 PM. When the alarm goes off, I stop and pray for ten minutes about one thing in particular that I am struggling with in my wellness plan or in my family. I pray about the same thing for ten days straight and record any insight in my prayer journal. At the end of those ten days, I move to another prayer request or petition.

Through the last few years, I have seen God do amazing things in my life through this practice.

Inner Reflection:. God is faithful and He hears my cry for help.

DAY 3 ~ MAKING PRAYER A PRIORITY

Let's begin our study time today by reading through James 5:13 one more time.

Now let's take time to write out our Scripture focus for this week.

"Therefore _______________ your _________ to each other and _________ for each other so that you may be _____________. The prayer of a _________________ person is _____________ and _____________." James 5:16

Our wellness journey should be about putting God first in our lives. When we begin to pray about the changes that need to take place, we allow God to be in charge. Through prayer He becomes the priority.

It's easy to be drawn into things of this world. A "me" society is prevalent today and putting God first doesn't fit the worldly view of things. Prayer is not an activity that we participate in, but a key that unlocks the door to God's work, God's energy, God's power, and God's strength.

How might it make a difference in your life if you allow God first in dealing with a healthy lifestyle? Explain.

____

____

____

Read 1 Corinthians 6:19.

What does it say about your body?

____

____

____

Who resides in your temple?

____

____

____

When I realized for the first time that I was a temple where the Holy Spirit resides, I broke down and wept. I realized I had been living in a sinful state in my body by allowing food to be first. That day I prayed, allowed the Lord to cleanse me, and began to view my body as the temple where the Holy Spirit really did live. No more trashing my temple with unhealthy food.

The Holy Spirit lives within you too. Your body is His home. Prioritizing Him first as you travel the wellness journey will make it joyful and exciting. What will you do to make Him first in your journey?

____

____

____

Inner Reflection: God is able to give me victory in all the areas in which I struggle.

DAY 4 ~ PRAYING AS I PREPARE TO DO MY PART

We need not think we can go to bed praying, "God make me thin, healthy, and rich," and then wake up an ideal size, have a perfect lab report, and have a fat bank account. Preparing is important on a daily basis. There is a great deal of peace and joy in having meals planned out, making a shopping list, following an exercise program, and living by a budget. Sounds great on paper, but making it happens takes a certain degree of praying and preparing.

I realize the day-to-day activities of my life are very important to my long-term success, but praying should always be the first thing on my game plan.

You may want to take some time this week to make a game plan for yourself or record your plan of action in your journal—but make a list of things you want God to do and then write down the things you need to do each day to keep your life in balance. Then spend some time each day with your list.

One of the first things that helped me get going was to make an appointment with my doctor. You might want to get a check-up and talk to your doctor about any health concerns, difficulty sleeping, or symptoms of depression you may have.

When was your last health check-up? _______________________________

Recording your food in a journal or using an online app will enable you to plan out your meals. Are you doing this consistently? Most important, are you being honest when writing down your food?

____

____

There's a difference between planning your meals in advance and rushing through, jotting down what you can remember eating.

Are you recording your food consumption as a planning tool?

____

____

My friend, Nancy Smith, always says we should view recording our food as a love letter to God. Being willing to write out our meals is being obedient to God. We have been learning through our study that God's love language is obedience, and it produces great joy even in the small things in this journey.

Preparing should involve your support circle. Who are those outside of your accountability group who encourage your efforts of preparing for a healthy lifestyle?

____

____

____

Enlist several close friends/family to be prayer warriors for you. Give them permission to help you stay in check with your eating. Remember to thank them for their support. I always say, "Give them permission to get up in your business."

Let's close today by looking up and writing out Ephesians 3:20.

____

____

____

Inner Reflection: Who are the people in my life willing to surround me with encouragement when I'm struggling and to hold me accountable for my food and exercise choices?

DAY 5 ~ PRAYING WITH COMPLETE JOY

Read John 15:11 and fill in the missing words.

"I have told you this so that _______ joy may be in you and that _________ joy may be complete."

Notice he says *my* joy. He wants to place His joy in you. His joy is steady; it doesn't come and go like the weather. His joy remains in you…it is complete and stable.

If you don't have joy in Jesus, your joy cannot be complete. How do you get this joy? A relationship with Him is like that of a branch to a vine. A branch is completely dependent upon a vine. It's the vine (Jesus), that produces fruit. We, being the branches, bear the fruit. If we want to see fruit at the end of our wellness program, what must we do?

____

____

____

When we begin to really believe what God says and stand on His promises, we meet Him, the Giver of Life and Joy, the one who makes all things new. Through this journey of faith, we are able to receive everything we need for life and righteousness from Him. He is full of life and joy to overflowing, and in the overflow we are able to find love, peace, and mercy.

Let's complete our study time today by writing out 2 Corinthians 3:18:

____

____

____

____

Allowing the Holy Spirit to fill our hearts and minds changes everything, including our relationship with Him. As we shift our hearts from a selfish attitude to casting every bit of our life before Him, we find He brings transformation and joy. It begins and ends with being dependent upon Him for the results of our efforts every day, day in and day out.

Complete joy comes as we pray to be transformed into His likeness. Through the precious blood of Jesus we are able to find hope, help, and healing. He enables us to count it all joy!

Inner Reflection: Jesus enables me to let go of all my hurts, hang-ups, and failures and press on in this journey of life, becoming all He desires for me to be.

DAY 6 ~ STOP AND CONSIDER

Let's begin our reflection time today by meditating on these two questions:

What is hindering you today?

What is keeping you from beginning your life-change process or completing your journey to the finish line?

Look up one of my favorite Scriptures, Hebrews 12:1. Take time to look it up in several Bible versions and find one that you relate to the most.

____

____

____

____

I want us to take some time today to consider the journey we are on. We are all walking/running a race of sorts through this life. As we reflect on this verse, it helps me realize it matters to God how I run the race.

In the early days of my life race, I did not pay too much attention to God's direction or decisions for my life. But over the last few years, I have come to realize that I can no longer ignore the flashing lights and warning signs. God's directions need to be heeded.

In our Scripture focus today, it says to throw off everything that hinders and the sin that so easily entangles. Let's begin by praying and asking God to reveal the things that are hindering us in our journey and the things that are sin.

Sins that are hindering my journey and stealing my joy:

____

____

____

____

____

People, places, or things that are hindering my journey and stealing my joy:

____

____

____

____

Our Scripture focus this week encourages us to confess our sins to each other. Do you have someone that you can talk to and share with? If not, you may want to make this a priority in your prayer life.

I have developed a model I would like to share with you to use for pressing on toward the goal that Christ Jesus has set before you. I begin each day in **PRAYER**.

P- Pray for the real power of Christ in my life today

R- Rest in God's strength to accomplish daily all that needs to be done

A- Accountability in this journey, pressing forward to freedom

Y- Yearning in my spirit for real freedom from bondage

E- Embracing with joy the changes of this new lifestyle and journey

R- Restoration of my body and soul, becoming who God created me to be

Take some time this week and use this model to spend some time in prayer with the Lord. Then take some time to listen for His voice and direction for your journey.

"Friends, I do not consider myself yet to have taken hold of it. But one thing I do: Forgetting what is behind and straining toward what is ahead, I press on toward the goal to win the prize for which God has called me heavenward in Christ Jesus." Philippians 3:13-14

CHOOSE YOUR CHALLENGE FOR THE WEEK

NUTRITION CHALLENGE—GOAL: CHANGE YOUR MIND!

Go back this week and review all the Nutrition Challenges you have taken through this study. Then answer the following questions. Remember, this is an exercise to help you grow!

1. Which challenge was the easiest for me? _________________ Why?

____

2. Which challenge was the hardest? _______________ Why?

____

3. What is the most interesting thing that I learned in the nutrition challenges? Did I have any revelations?

____

____

FITNESS CHALLENGE—GOAL: CHANGE YOUR BODY!

What has been the most life-changing thing I have learned through the fitness challenges during this study?

____

____

____

____

LIFESTYLE CHALLENGE—GOAL: CHANGE YOUR LIFE!

Someone once asked, if you don't set a goal, how will you know where you are going and how will you know when you arrive? A goal is like a contract with yourself. It drives your motivation. Set your goals realistically so that you can be successful.

HERE ARE SOME TIPS FOR SETTING GOALS:

- Write down your goal. Post it where you will see it often.
- Make the goal attainable. "I will exercise at least three times a week."
- Let everyone know about your goal and get people to encourage you.
- Reward your success on reaching your goal, but don't do it with food. This is one of the toughest places to retrain yourself, because most of us have been rewarded with food from the time we were sitting in a highchair.

What week of the Lifestyle Challenges has made the most impact on my life over the last ten weeks?

____

Why?

____

____

CHALLENGE I CHOSE ~ PROGRESS I MADE:

DAY 7 ~ JOURNAL PROMPT

Today, Lord, my cry to You looks like…

POSITIVE AFFIRMATIONS

Change your thoughts DAILY—with affirmations on God's Word!

I am beautiful, capable, and lovable. I am valuable.

I love myself unconditionally and nurture myself in every way.

I am unique, the apple of God's eye.

I am a child of God.

I love people and show love, warmth, and friendship to all.

I am healed of all my childhood wounds, and I hold no account of wrong done to me.

I can be intimate with myself and others.

All of my relationships are based on integrity and respect.

I am intelligent and have great creativity. I can concentrate easily.

I can analyze and solve problems.

I learn quickly and have an excellent memory.

I have the mind of Christ. I can make decisions with confidence.

I am diligent, faithful, and have a spirit of excellence.

Whatever I put my hand to will prosper.

God always causes me to triumph in Christ.

I let go of things I cannot control.

I have the courage to change the things I should change, the serenity to accept the things I cannot change, and the wisdom to know the difference.

I have no need to control people or situations.

I am controlled by the Holy Spirit.

I am a success. I can do anything I put my mind to.

I can do all things through Christ, who strengthens me.

I see each day as a new and positive adventure.

I give thanks in all things.

I express my potential more and more each day.

I see problems as exciting challenges that cause me to grow stronger and stronger in my faith.

I visualize myself as the person God wants me to be.

I see myself achieving my goals and fulfilling God's purpose for my life.

I live every day with passion and power.

I feel strong, excited, passionate, and powerful.

I feel tremendous confidence. I have all the abilities I need to succeed.

Every cell in my body vibrates with health, healing, vitality, and love.

I am healthy and strong and filled with vitality.

Jesus took every sickness and every disease away from me.

I awaken each day feeling healthy and alive with energy.

Any tension I feel is simply a signal to relax, release, and let go.

I always have more than enough energy to do all I want to do.

All that I am, I derive from Jesus.

He is always in my thoughts, and I pray without ceasing.

Jesus is my strength, my joy, my peace.

He is with me wherever I go, and He promised never to leave me or forsake me.

I surrender my life to Jesus Christ.

I have a wonderful, fulfilling relationship with Jesus.

I trust my conscience, which is led by the Holy Spirit.

I feel God's presence at all times.

I walk in the fruit of the Spirit of love, joy, peace, patience, goodness, gentleness, faith, meekness, and self-control.

I am sustained by the love of Christ. The peace of God rests upon me.

I do not worry about anything.

In everything, I give thanks to God and give my cares to Him.

The peace that passes understanding guards my heart and mind, and I remain calm no matter what happens around me.

ABOUT—JOYCE AINSWORTH

After struggling with being overweight for most of her life, Joyce's personal weight-loss story is powerful! Not only has she lost over 150 pounds, but she has learned the importance of "true health" and the benefits of maintaining this healthy lifestyle that include a healthy mind, body, and spirit.

Joyce's desire to help others find "true health" has fueled her passion and drive to become a Certified Personal Trainer through the International Sports Sciences Association (ISSA). She has also earned a Specialization in Fitness Nutrition (SFN) through the ISSA. She is TRX Qualified and holds a Certificate of Completion in Training the Bariatric Client through the Kinesis Center.

Joyce can attest that nutrition and physical fitness are components of a healthy lifestyle! She is a member of the IDEA Health and Fitness Association, AWSA (Advanced Writers and Speakers Association), and an Auxiliary with the Gideon's International.

Joyce is a writer, speaker, and a successful business owner. She is the author of four books: *Food, Freedom and Finish Lines! How to Lose the Weight and Win Back Your Life*, *Nutrition For Life~ Food and Fitness Tips for Success*, *Retracing Your History with Food ~ Workbook for Emotional Mapping*, and a cookbook, *Simply Healthy Recipes ~ Food for the Body and Soul*.

Joyce currently works as a personal trainer, conducts workshops and cooking demonstrations, and speaks at seminars, conferences, and other types of events across the country. She teaches classes at her local church and also works part-time with a Senior Support Ministry for the Elderly.

Regardless of age or fitness level, benefits of a healthy lifestyle and proper nutrition and balance can be achieved. As we develop a strong mind, body and spirit, a positive outlook on life, and deep inner confidence, we find that life change really is possible.

If you are interested in talking with Joyce about some life changing possibilities, please contact her at 601-927-8974 or e-mail her at glenna@netdoor.com.

ABOUT—JUNE CHAPKO

June Chapko, a transplanted Texan since 1958, resides in San Antonio with her husband Nick and Shih Tzu puppy, Chai. She is a mom, grandmother, and great-grandmother. She enjoys reading, quilting, and finding teacup treasures for her burgeoning collection.

June is a member of American Christian Fiction Writers and AWSA (Advanced Writers and Speakers Association). June is certified as a CLASS speaker. She has written two healthy living Bible studies, many devotionals, and has been published in *Mature Living*, *Quilt World Magazines*, and other publications.

Her two novels, *The Estate Sale* and *Legacy's Path* are the first in her Legacy series, with the third due out in spring of 2021.

June is active in her church women's ministry and teaches a women's Sunday school class. She developed a small group Spiritual Journaling workshop which she has led at retreats and in her church.

For more information about inviting June to speak at your women's event, or for a list of her speaking topics, please contact her at 210-359-8493 or email chapkoj@aol.com.

During the writing of this book, June was unaware of a tumor growing in her breast. Shortly after completion of the manuscript she was given a diagnosis of stage 2 breast cancer. June states, "I believe that God used the material in this Bible study to enable me to find joy in my cancer journey. He changed my mind from fear to faith and trials to trust, the kind only He can provide." June is currently planning a devotional book for breast cancer patients in need of real joy during their journey to wellness through faith in God. She hopes to have it out in summer of 2021.